International Dimensions of

Information Systems and Technology

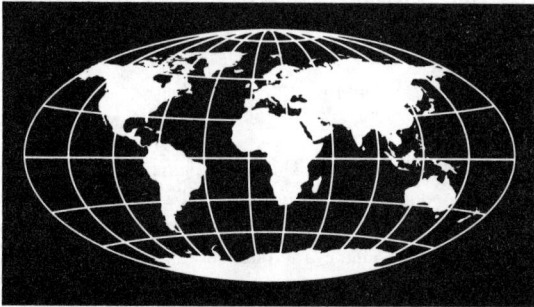

P. Candace Deans
Wake Forest University

Michael J. Kane
University of Kentucky

THE KENT INTERNATIONAL DIMENSIONS OF BUSINESS SERIES
David A. Ricks—*Series Consulting Editor*

PWS-KENT PUBLISHING COMPANY
Boston

Dedicated to

*Colleagues in the School of Business and Accountancy
at Wake Forest University
and
Jennifer Kane and the entire Kane Family*

PWS-KENT
Publishing Company

20 Park Plaza
Boston, Massachusetts 02116

Editor: Rolf Janke
Assistant Editor: Kathleen Tibbetts
Production Editor: Kirby Lozyniak
Text/Cover Designer: Julie Gecha
Manufacturing Coordinator: Lisa Flanagan
Text Printer/Binder: Courier/Westford

PWS-KENT Publishing Company is a division of Wadsworth, Inc.

Printed in the United States of America
1 2 3 4 5 6 7 8 9 — 97 96 95 94 93 92

Library of Congress Cataloging-in-Publication Data

Deans, P. Candace.
    International dimensions of information systems and technology / P. Candace Deans, Michael J. Kane.
    p. cm. —(The Kent international dimensions of business series)
    Includes bibliographical references and index.
    ISBN 0-534-92811-0
    1. Information resources management.   2. Computer networks.
    I. Kane, Michael J.   II. Title.   III. Series.
T58.64.D43   1992
658.4'038—dc20

91-39196
CIP

Series Foreword

Prior to World War II, the number of firms involved in foreign direct investment was relatively small. Although several U.S. companies were obtaining raw materials from other countries, most firms were only interested in the U.S. market. This changed, however, during the 1950s—especially after the creation of the European Economic Community. Since that time, there has been a rapid expansion in international business activity.

The majority of the world's large corporations now perform an increasing proportion of their business activities outside of their home countries. For many of these companies, international business returns over one-half of their profits, and it is becoming more and more common for a typical corporation to earn at least one-fourth of its profits through international business involvement. In fact, it is now rather rare for any large firm not to be a participant in the world of international business.

International business is of great importance in most countries and that importance continues to grow. To meet the demand for increased knowledge in this area, business schools are attempting to add international dimensions to their curricula. Faculty members are becoming more interested in teaching a greater variety of international business courses and are striving to add international dimensions to other courses. Students, aware of the increasing probability that they will be employed by firms engaged in international business activities, are seeking knowledge of the problem-solving techniques unique to international business. As the American Assembly of Collegiate Schools of Business has observed, however, there is a shortage of information available. Most business textbooks do not adequately consider the international dimensions of business and much of the supplemental material is disjointed, overly narrow, or otherwise inadequate in the classroom.

This series has been developed to overcome such problems. The books are written by some of the most respected authors in the various areas of international business. Each author is extremely well known in the Academy of International

Business and in his or her other professional academies. They possess an outstanding knowledge of their own subject matter and a talent for explaining it.

These books, in which the authors have identified the most important international aspects of their fields, have been written in a format that facilitates their use as supplemental material in business courses.

The Kent International Dimensions of Business Series offers a unique and much needed opportunity to bring international dimensions of business into the classroom. The series has been developed by leaders in the field after years of discussion and careful consideration and the timely encouragement and support provided by the PWS-KENT staff on this project. I am proud to be associated with this series and highly recommend it to you.

David A. Ricks
Consulting Editor to the
Kent International Dimensions of Business Series
Professor of International Business,
University of South Carolina

Preface

As we move toward the next century, information technology will play an increasingly significant role in a rapidly evolving interdependent international economy. For the corporation of the future in a worldwide marketplace, information systems and technology will provide the communications infrastructure for decision support and essential links with buyers, suppliers, customers, and strategic alliances. Currently, many businesses such as the airlines and financial institutions rely heavily on connections to a global information network. To compete globally, companies will continue to look to information technology to manage complexity and rapid change in an unpredictable international business world.

Business school curricula must be responsive to the demands of a business environment that has become increasingly international, more information driven, and more service oriented. A global marketplace requires that students be educated with a broader base of knowledge. Although extensive curriculum material has been developed that addresses the international dimensions of marketing, accounting, finance, and management, very few resources are available that address the international dimensions of information systems. Internationalization of the information systems and technology curriculum is beginning to receive increased attention by those in the field. There is clearly an increasing demand for supplemental material that addresses relevant international information systems and technology issues. Current business trends certainly indicate that this topic will gain increased significance in the future.

This book represents the first step toward addressing this particular need of the academic community. The topics covered reflect the state-of-the-art knowledge in this area. On many issues, little international research has been reported, while in other areas no research has been done at all. The multidisciplinary aspects of information systems and technology make integration of the issues and topics difficult. We have attempted to contribute in a small way by integrating related issues and topics in international business, strategic management, information systems, and technology. Although there are many limitations, quite a bit of research is currently in progress and the quest for knowledge in this area is evolving. Clearly, this is an exciting and rapidly growing field of study.

This book can be used as a supplement to an introductory management information systems (MIS) course at either the undergraduate or graduate level. It may also be used as a supplement for courses in international management or management of technology. Further, this book can be used as the core text for an international information systems course that is supported with additional readings. It is also intended that the practitioner find this book of value.

The authors would like to express special appreciation to a mutual mentor, Dr. David A. Ricks. He provided support and encouragement for work that addresses the interface of two very different streams of research: international business and management information systems. His vision and encouragement in an area that at the time was virtually void of any literature has never wavered. It is interesting today to look back at how little was known when we began this journey, and how much has been discovered in the process and yet see that so much is still to be uncovered.

There are also others who have made their own special contributions. In particular, Candace Deans would like to thank Kirk Karwan, Martin Goslar, Brian Toyne, Bob Markland, and Dean James F. Kane at the University of South Carolina for their contributions and support of her research in this area. She also extends appreciation to Dean Thomas C. Taylor, of the School of Business and Accountancy, and Julie Cole, Director of Research and Sponsored Programs, both of Wake Forest University. An additional note of thanks to Buddy Zincone, Associate Dean of the School of Business at East Carolina University, whose support and encouragement go back many years.

Mike Kane wishes to thank Dean Richard W. Furst at the University of Kentucky and his former colleagues at IBM, particularly James Ransco and David Mims. He also extends appreciation to Dean Kane and the international business faculty of the University of South Carolina.

Finally, the authors would like to thank the staff at PWS-KENT and Kathleen Tibbetts, in particular, for continued encouragement. For her enthusiastic assistance in preparing the manuscript we would like to thank Suzanne Pribble at the University of Kentucky's International Business Center. We also extend appreciation for the helpful suggestions of the reviewers of this manuscript:

Elias Awad, *University of Virginia;* **Gordon Davis,** *University of Minnesota;* **David V. Gibson,** *The University of Texas at Austin;* **Luis R. Gomez-Mejia,** *Arizona State University;* **Ido Millet,** *Bentley College.*

P. Candace Deans
Michael J. Kane

About the Authors

Candace Deans is Assistant Professor of Management Information Systems at Wake Forest University. She earned her Ph.D. degree from the University of South Carolina with a major in management information systems and minor in international business. Her current research activities focus on international information systems issues. She has published articles on this topic in the *Journal of Management Information Systems* and the *Journal of High Technology Management Research*. She is a member of the Academy of International Business, the International Academy for Information Management, the Society for Information Management, the Information Resource Management Association, the Decision Sciences Institute, and the Institute of Management Science.

Michael J. Kane is Assistant Research Professor of International Business at the University of Kentucky, where he is also the Director of the U.S.-Japan International Management Institute, and Associate Director of the International Business Center. Prior to entering academia, he held several field and marketing management positions with IBM's National Accounts Division in the United States and the Asia/Pacific Group headquartered in Tokyo, Japan. He is frequently cited in the *Wall Street Journal, Business Week, The Economist,* and many other publications on a variety of Japanese and international business-related issues. Professor Kane is the recipient of numerous grants from foundations, private industries, and government agencies to conduct research and develop educational programs in international business. His research appears in the *Journal of International Business Studies* and the *Columbia Journal of World Business.*

Contents

Chapter **THREE**

A Closer Look at International Influences on IS Function: Service MNCs Versus Manufacturing MNCs   40

Chapter **FOUR**

Transnational Flows of Data and Information   64

Chapter **FIVE**

International Telecommunications and Global Connectivity   93

Chapter **EIGHT**

Chapter ONE

Information Systems Management: The Global Perspective

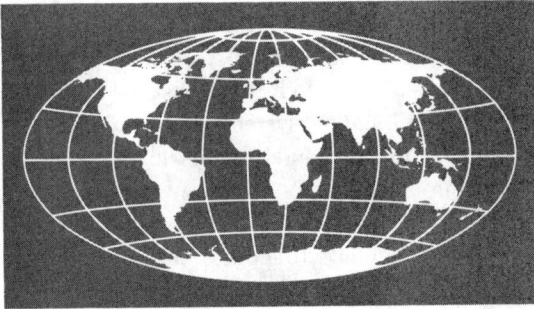

Two major forces currently transforming business today are globalization of the marketplace and the impact of information technology on the firm. The important link between these two major forces is information. Today, power is in information. The organization of the 1990s can no longer ignore the importance of information, both as a strategic resource and as a potential means by which to obtain competitive advantage. Information technology is gaining significant attention not only as a catalyst that is driving the global marketplace but also as a solution base from which to address international managerial challenges. In the international operating environment, the firm's information systems will provide the strongest link in this business chain of partners, products, suppliers, and customers. As never before, the firm will rely on its

1

information systems to maintain its competitive position in a rapidly changing global marketplace.

William G. McGowan, chairman of the International Communications Association, strongly believes that the decade of the 1990s will be recognized as the period in history when international business and global telecommunications got their act together.[1] We will see an acceleration of trends that have slowly developed over the past twenty years and are now working together to create today's interdependent international economy. Technological change is taking place so rapidly that it is difficult to keep abreast of new advancements. Companies that equip themselves with information technologies to do business around the clock and around the world will thrive in this rapidly evolving global marketplace.[2]

According to a recent report prepared by IBM,[3] a common thought among many key business executives today is that cooperation, especially in the international context, will be necessary to gain a competitive edge in the future. In essence, many top executives feel that future successful competitors will be those that make the critical decision to cooperate. Through joint ventures and partnerships, companies will find new opportunities and markets that would be otherwise too difficult or expensive to attain. The firm's information systems will play a significant role as executives respond to the demands of this challenging and changing global business environment.

The technological advancements that are shrinking the globe and creating the reality of a global village are only beginning. By the next century, we can predict with confidence that technological advancements will draw together the people of this world as never before in history.[4] Business may be viewed as international with a domestic component. The worldwide communications infrastructure will likely become as significant as our transportation infrastructure. Advancements in information technology will change the meaning of the word *foreign* as people, goods, and services from all parts of the world routinely mix together. Tomorrow's concepts of international borders, diverse cultures, and political systems will likely not be what they have been in this century.[5]

INTERNATIONAL BUSINESS AND THE MULTINATIONAL CORPORATION

International business has been defined in many ways by different authors. For our purposes, we will define international business in a broad sense to include any business activity that crosses national borders.

Unique obstacles, challenges, and opportunities may emerge as a result of operating in more than one country. A major component of international business activity involves the impact of environmental influences on both the corporation and the corporation's influence on its international environment. We will discuss these environmental influences in more detail in Chapter 2.

Both international business and management information systems (MIS) are grounded firmly in the field of management. As stated by Robock and Simmonds, international business is recognized as a field of management training that "deals with business activities that cross national boundaries, whether they be movement of goods, services, capital, or personnel; transfers of technology, information or data; or even the supervision of employees."[6] The growth of business transactions across national borders and the resulting complexity of these transactions gave rise to unique management problems. Education in management training to address these special problems provided the impetus and need for a separate field of study. Likewise, as Dickson, Benbasat, and King point out, the most significant origins of MIS go back to the field of management.[7] MIS emerged as a separate branch of management in response to new and unique management problems associated with the increased importance of information to the organization and the complexities associated with the development of information systems to support the various functions of the firm. The information systems (IS) function can no longer be viewed as an isolated entity within the organization. Rather, for the multinational corporation (MNC), the firm's information systems will provide the global link with subsidiaries, suppliers, customers, and competitors.

We will use the term *multinational corporation* to refer to any firm that has one or more foreign affiliates or production facilities and is therefore involved in international management. A firm may be involved in international business through exporting or importing and not be recognized as a multinational firm. Companies involved primarily with exporting and importing may certainly encounter unique concerns in transferring data and information across national borders. In this book, however, we will concentrate on international issues from the perspective of the multinational firm.

The definition that will be used for *information systems technology* (IT) will be the same as that used by Cash, McFarlan, and McKenney and will include the technologies of computers, telecommunications, and office automation.[8] In our discussions of the firm's information systems, we will generally use the term *information systems* (IS) to clearly encompass the transaction processing level. We will not, however, make a formal distinction between IS and MIS.

DOMESTIC VERSUS INTERNATIONAL BUSINESS

Since international business is recognized as an extension of the firm's domestic business operations, MNCs may face unique problems, challenges and opportunities not necessarily encountered by a domestic firm. The international transfer and management of information systems technology is also more complex due to the variety of cultures, governments, legal systems, and environments in which these firms operate. Managing the information resource in an international context is a difficult task and one that deserves considerable attention.

As emphasized by Korth, the international business environment is composed of the same elements as the domestic environment (governmental, legal, cultural, and economic). As shown in Figure 1–1, many of these factors are constants in the domestic (U.S.) environment (for example, a single language, a common currency, a reasonably homogeneous culture, and a well-developed infrastructure). In the international business environment, however, there are many constraints that cannot be ignored and potential differences that may vary depending upon the location of the firm's international business operations.[9] Throughout this book we will concentrate on those issues that make the management of the firm's information systems and information technology more difficult internationally than domestically.

EVOLUTION OF THE MULTINATIONAL ENTERPRISE

Companies do not typically become multinational enterprises overnight. With some exceptions, most firms follow an evolutionary path in their development into a multinational organization. The factors contributing to this evolution are both internal and external. Internal factors may include the firm's strategic orientation, the vision of key executives, and the history of the firm. External factors such as the firm's industry, competition, and governmental influence also contribute to this evolution.

In Chapter 6, we will discuss in detail the evolution of the multinational enterprise from the perspective of the firm's strategic business

---

Domestic Environment

- Single language
- Common currency
- Reasonably homogeneous culture
- Well-developed infrastructure
- One government—one body of regulations
- Single geographic entity—limited time zones

International Environment

- Multilingual
- Multicultural
- Multigovernments
- Multiregulations
- Multiple geographic entities
- Multiple time zones
- Multiple currencies

FIGURE 1-1   Domestic Business Versus International Business

operations and accompanying information systems requirements. As a brief introduction, Figure 1–2 depicts the evolution of the multinational enterprise as a series of five steps or stages.

As Figure 1–2 shows, the evolution of the multinational enterprise involves a progressive increase in the level of capital investment abroad and operational complexity. As the firm develops from exporting to global integration, the percentage of the firm's total capital invested in plant, equipment, personnel, and materials overseas becomes very large. At the same time, the level of complexity inherent in the operations increases substantially, requiring the firm to structure and manage its international organization accordingly.

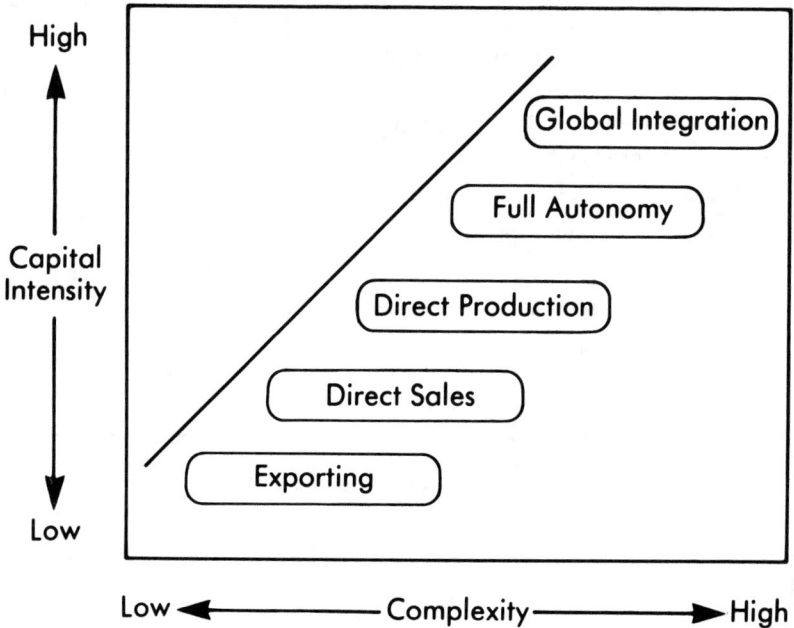

FIGURE 1-2   The Evolution of the Multinational Enterprise

Exporting

Many firms establish their international business operations as the result of an unsolicited order from abroad. As these orders begin to grow, the firm may assign someone in the marketing department to handle the fulfillment of these orders. If the volume of overseas orders continues to grow, the firm may organize a separate export department or establish overseas distributors and/or licensed marketing agents. As the percentage of international sales increases and the number of export countries expands, senior management may want more direct control over the marketing operations abroad.

Direct Sales

The second stage of the evolution moves the firm into direct sales, through which the firm's own employees market in each foreign country. This stage is evidenced by the establishment of a foreign sales office or branch location. Typically, the office is staffed by foreign nationals but may include an expatriate manager from the firm's headquarters. The primary benefits of a foreign, direct-sales capability are two-fold: first, the profit margins are greater because the firm can eliminate the middle distributor and agent; second, the firm can gain valuable first-hand knowledge about the overseas marketplace.

It is not unusual for the firm to face competition from local firms who have developed similar products. In fact, the local firm may have an advantage because it can both manufacture and sell in that country. If manufacturing costs are lower in that country, it is also possible that the foreign firm may begin creating competition in the home market.

Direct Production

To stay competitive, the company may invest in overseas production facilities. In this stage of the evolution, the firm increases its level of investment and must manage both marketing and production functions in two or more countries.

Full Autonomy

The fourth stage in the evolution is full autonomy. If the countries in which the firm is doing business represent substantially large markets, or governments and competitive pressures demand such a move, the company may establish fully autonomous subsidiaries that control the entire business in each country. The international operations of the firm can be viewed as a portfolio of independent country businesses, each with its own president and board of directors.

Global Integration

If the firm continues to grow in many markets around the world, it will increasingly see the advantage of globally coordinating its operations so that it can gain the advantages of economies of scale and scope. However, global integration is very complex and requires a very sophisticated organizational structure and information systems infrastructure.

TYPES OF INTERNATIONAL BUSINESS ACTIVITY

Based on these stages in the development of the multinational firm, we can specify different types of international business operations. As discussed, the multinational corporation may engage exclusively in exporting or importing, may produce some goods and services abroad but remain essentially domestically based, or may value its international operations equally to or more than its domestic ones.[10] Firms that are considered truly global no longer give their domestic operations higher priority than their international operations. The domestic component no longer dominates even though the firm may have a strong domestic interest. It is clear, however, that the concerns specific to the firm's IS function in the multinational corporation will depend to a large degree upon the importance of foreign markets in the firm's overall strategy.

Authors have described international business activities in a variety of ways. For the purposes of our discussions, we use the same classification as Korth and describe the activities in the following paragraphs.

Exports and Imports of Goods and Services

Exporting and importing of either merchandise or services represent the simplest forms of international business activity. Foreign trade usually represents the initial phase of international business activity for most firms.

Exports and Imports of Portfolio Capital

Portfolio investment is closely related to other types of exports and imports. Flows of capital may include the purchase or sale of marketable securities, nonsecurity-type financial investments, and noncontrolling common stock. An important characteristic of this type of international activity is that it does not usually involve direct overseas management.

Direct Investment

Foreign direct investment is recognized as the most complicated form of international business activity because it involves actual ownership of foreign operations and direct participation in the management of the foreign investment. Cooperative arrangements involving joint ventures or ventures with the foreign government as a partner are common in international business activities of this nature.

THE IMPORTANCE OF THE INTERNATIONAL DIMENSION

In today's business world, every firm operates in an international environment and is affected by trends, events, and conditions that are occurring outside the United States. The last two decades have witnessed an explosive growth in the number and size of U.S. and foreign multinationals. The strictly domestic (U.S.) firm with little or no international involvement can no longer enjoy the luxury of ignoring its global competitors. It is becoming increasingly important for U.S. firms to be concerned about business beyond the U.S. marketplace both for competitive reasons as well as for identifying opportunities for growth and increased market share for its products and services.

Top executives predict that by the turn of the century, companies' choices of leaders will be affected by increased international competition, globalization of companies, advancements in technology, and the speed of overall change. The chief executives of the next century will need multienvironment, multicountry, multifunctional, and possibly multicompany and multi-industry experience. The changing business environment will demand a different type of chief executive officer (CEO). By the year 2000, it will likely be hard to find a chief executive who doesn't routinely receive information electronically locally, nationally, and internationally.[11] Change will be an inevitable part of doing business in the decade ahead.

Multinational managers are changing their priorities as they increasingly tackle the task of simultaneously optimizing efficiency, responsiveness, and learning in their worldwide operations.[12] MNCs that have in the past been successful with one-dimensional strategies are now being forced to broaden their outlooks. What is now critical is a managerial mindset that recognizes the need for multidimensional strategies, views problems from both local and global perspectives, and accepts the importance of flexibility in its management approaches.[13]

THE ROLE OF INFORMATION TECHNOLOGY IN THE EVOLVING GLOBAL MARKETPLACE

Information technology is changing the way we do business. Already, information technology enables us to operate in a paperless office. Networks provide the foundation for this capability. As we enter the age of the network it will be possible to support many forms of information exchange including voice, data, graphics, facsimile, videoconferencing, electronic mail, voice messaging, and integrated combinations of all these.[14] The challenges posed by these opportunities in an international context still lie ahead.

Successful implementations of information technologies in a domestic context will be transferred to the firm's international operations. Recognizing that cultural, economic, political, legal, and technological barriers may dictate the extent to which various IS technologies are appropriate, information technology may offer tremendous opportunities for the firm's international operations. On an international scale, MNCs have taken advantage of teleconferencing to replace travel, videoconferencing to provide interactive training for geographically distant locations, facsimile in lieu of the postal systems, and electronic mail to replace the phone system. Information technology has the potential to help overcome barriers to international business activity such as time zone differences, geographic restrictions, and language and cultural constraints. Global e-mail, for example, has provided the MNC with a valuable tool for working around time zone differences.[15] As Porter and Millar emphasize, companies that anticipate the power of information technology will be at a competitive advantage, while those that do not respond may be forced to accept changes initiated by others.[16]

Information technology is providing the means by which to lay the foundation for an international information highway system. From anywhere in the U.S., it is now possible to deal with business associates in a Tokyo office as if you were in the same room sharing documents and conversations.[17] We are fast moving toward the reality of a single worldwide information network capable of communicating data, voice, text, or image anywhere in the world.

INFORMATION SYSTEMS: THE GLOBAL COMMUNICATIONS LINK

Multinational corporate executives tend to agree that from an information-sharing perspective, it is necessary to operate as a single global operation rather than as a series of independent geographic entities.[18] Coordinating the firm's activities at many sites in various countries requires good information sharing and communication. Global companies rely totally on their information systems to provide this communication infrastructure to support the business operations, functions, and decision-making activities of the firm. In order to grow internationally, these operations must be integrated into corporate information flows and strategies. To meet these challenges, multinationals are rethinking their information systems networks as they continually strive to service global customers on a global basis.[19]

Peter Drucker refers to the organization of the future as an information-based organization. Advancements in information technology are moving the firm from a data level to an information level. As this process takes place, decision-making activities, the structure of management, and the manner in which work is accomplished begins to be transformed. This process is already occurring quite rapidly in many companies around the world. To remain competitive and possibly even to survive, the business organization of the future will have little choice but to become information-based. Building this information-based organization is what Drucker refers to as the managerial challenge of the future.[20]

SUMMARY AND OVERVIEW

This first chapter provides an overview and appreciation of the significance of international business activity and the role of the firm's information systems in the evolving global marketplace. As we continue to move toward a more integrated world economy, it will become increasingly important to incorporate these dimensions into the study of information systems.

The international business operating environment represents added levels of complexity and unique concerns that must be considered as the firm progresses in its development as a multinational organization. Typically, the multinational firm moves through a series of stages, from exporting to global integration. Capital invested abroad and operational complexity increase substantially as the firm moves along this continuum.

Information technology provides the means by which the MNC can better integrate its global operations. Recognizing that many obstacles still exist, advancements in information technology provide the multinational firm with many alternatives and options not before available. As emphasized in this chapter, the firm's information systems and technology will play a significant role in future global business operations.

In Chapter 2, we will concentrate more specifically on the environmental factors that may influence the firm's IS function. In this context, we will focus on those issues relevant to the domestic, foreign, and international environments of which the IS function is a part. An overview of important IS issues will be incorporated into this framework.

In Chapter 3, attention will be directed toward international variables that affect the IS function in the context of differences between multinational service and manufacturing firms. We will examine general international variables as well as the firm's international organizational characteristics.

Chapters 4 and 5 will be devoted to the technological dimensions that must be addressed on an international scale. The focus of Chapter 4 will be on international transfers of data and information. Chapter 5 will be directed toward those issues most relevant to international telecommunications and global connectivity.

Managerial issues specific to the transfer and infusion of IS technology on an international scale will be addressed in chapters 6 and 7. In Chapter 6, those issues most relevant to planning for the firm's international information systems will be discussed. Strategic implications of information technology on a global scale will be introduced in Chapter 7.

In the final chapter, we will discuss what we foresee as some of the future directions and significant developments currently taking place for IS in the international arena.

NOTES

1. William G. McGowan, "Why Global?" *Telecommunications* (April 1989): S–6.
2. Ibid.
3. *IBM Update*, U.S. Marketing and Services, International Business Machines Corporation (January 1990), 1.
4. Ibid.
5. Ibid.
6. Stefan H. Robock and Kenneth Simmonds, *International Business and the Multinational Enterprise* (Illinois: Richard D. Irwin, 1983), 3.
7. G. W. Dickson, I. Benbasat, and W. R. King, "The MIS Area: Problems, Challenges and Opportunities," *Data Base* (Winter 1982): 7–12.
8. James I. Cash, Jr., Warren F. McFarlan, and James L. McKenney, *Corporate Information Systems Management* (Illinois: Richard D. Irwin, 1988), 1.
9. Christopher M. Korth, *International Business Environment and Management* (New Jersey: Prentice Hall, Inc., 1985), 4.
10. Ibid., 11–12.
11. Amanda Bennett, "The Chief Executives in the Year 2000 Will Be Experienced Abroad," *Wall Street Journal* (February 27, 1989): 1.
12. Christopher A. Bartlett and Sumantra Goshal, "Managing Across Borders: New Strategic Requirements," *Sloan Management Review* (Summer 1987): 7–17.

13. Christopher A. Bartlett and Sumantra Goshal, "Managing Across Borders: New Organizational Responses," *Sloan Management Review* (Fall 1987): 43–53.

14. *IBM Update,* 13.

15. Janet Fiderio, "Information Must Conform in a World Without Borders," *Computerworld* (October 1990): 91–95.

16. Michael E. Porter and Victor E. Millar, "How Information Gives You Competitive Advantage," *Harvard Business Review* (March–April 1979): 137–145.

17. John Nasbitt and Patricia Aburdene, *Ten New Directions for the 1990s Megatrends 2000* (New York: William Morrow & Company, Inc., 1990), 23.

18. Fiderio, 91.

19. Ibid., 93.

20. Peter F. Drucker, "The Coming of the New Organization," *Harvard Business Review* (January–February 1988): 45–53.

STUDY QUESTIONS

1. Discuss some of the variables that make domestic business different from international business.

2. Describe the typical pattern by which a domestic firm evolves to the status of a multinational enterprise. Why is the evolution increasingly capital intensive and complex?

3. Discuss some of the reasons for studying the international dimensions relevant to the firm's information systems function.

4. How is information technology changing the way we do business, both domestically and on an international scale?

5. Discuss what you think Peter Drucker means when he refers to the future firm as an information-based organization?

SUGGESTED READINGS

Carlyle, Ralph Emmett. "Managing IS at Multinationals." *Datamation* (March 1987): 54–66.

Contractor, Farok J., and Peter Lorange, eds. *Cooperative Strategies in International Business.* Massachusetts: D. C. Heath, 1988.

Diebold, John. *Business in the Age of Information.* New York: Amacom, 1985.

Feather, Frank. *G-Forces: The 35 Global Forces Restructuring Our Future.* New York: William Morrow & Co., 1989.

Gomes-Casseres, Benjamin. "Joint Ventures in the Face of Global Competition." *Sloan Management Review* (Spring 1989): 17–26.

Hammer, Michael, and Glenn E. Mangurian. "The Changing Value of Communications Technology." *Sloan Management Review* (Winter 1987): 65–71.

Hax, Arnoldo C. "Building the Firm of the Future." *Sloan Management Review* (Spring 1989): 75–82.

Horton, Robert. "Future Challenges to Management." *MIT Management* (Winter 1989): 3–6.

Kiplinger, Austin H., and Knight A. Kiplinger. *America in the Global '90s.* Washington, D.C.: Kiplinger Washington Editors, 1989.

Leveson, Irving. *American Challenges: Business and Government in the World of the 1990s.* New York: Praeger, 1991.

Marchand, Donald A. "IRM Interview: Fred H. Lambrou." *Information Management Review* (Spring 1987): 81–91.

———. "IRM Interview: Peter G. W. Keen." *Information Management Review* (Winter 1989): 65–75.

———. "IRM Interview: John Diebold." *Information Management Review* (Summer 1988): 71–79.

Marchand, Donald A., and H. W. Horton. *Infotrends.* New York: Wiley, 1986.

Ohmae, Kenichi. "Managing in a Borderless World." *Harvard Business Review* (May–June 1989): 152–161.

———. *The Borderless World.* New York: Harper Business/Harper Collins, 1990.

Prahalad, C. K., and Yves Doz. *The Multinational Mission: Balancing Local Demands and Global Vision.* New York: Free Press, 1987.

Rockart, John F., and James E. Short. "IT in the 1990s: Managing Organizational Interdependence." *Sloan Management Review* (Winter 1989): 7–17.

Zuboff, Shoshana. *In the Age of the Smart Machine: the Future of Work and Power.* New York: Basic Books, 1988.

Chapter TWO

International Environmental Influences on the Information Systems Function

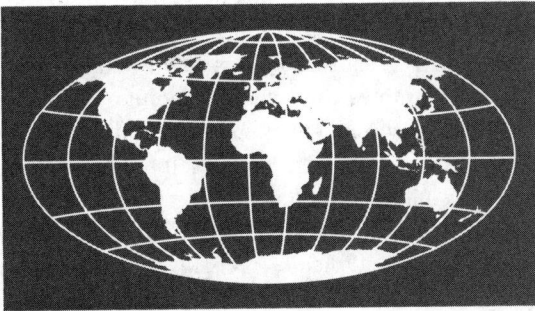

International environmental forces represent the sum of all factors that affect the direction and success of the firm's international business operations. It is clear that the IS function within the MNC is influenced by added dimensions and unique variables that a comparable, strictly domestic U.S. firm would not encounter. Decision making becomes more complex because multiple variables and interacting forces must now be considered.

In this chapter we will begin by discussing the international environment from the perspective of the international manager. From this broad discussion, we will then concentrate on the international environmental forces most relevant to the firm's IS function. In particular, international information systems issues recognized as most important for the MNC will be discussed in the context of the firm's domestic, international, and foreign environments.

THE INTERNATIONAL MANAGEMENT ENVIRONMENT

Environmental influences may be thought of from the broad perspective of international management in general. In this context, international management includes both the coordination of the firm's human and physical resources as well as the monitoring of environmental impacts on the firm.[1] International managers of specific functional areas, product areas, or geographic areas will necessarily focus on a more limited set of relevant variables specific to their task at hand. As discussed in Chapter 1, both the MIS and international business fields of study have their origins in management. It is, therefore, appropriate that we first discuss the total international environment of management before we focus specifically on those dimensions most relevant to the firm's information systems. Compared to the domestic manager, the international manager is faced with a more complex environment that includes an array of additional variables that must be monitored.

The international environment encompasses all environments of each nation in which the firm does business. Each nation's environment consists of four basic components that include legal, cultural, economic, and political dimensions. In Table 2–1, Phatak has summarized the most significant variables typically recognized for each of these environmental components. Clearly, the multinational manager must deal with a complex set of elements that may become even more complicated depending upon the number of countries in which the firm operates and the locations of its foreign affiliates. Our focus is on those factors that specifically affect business activity and the multinational firm.

From the perspective of the *economic* environment, there are two dimensions that must be considered by multinational managers. First, the domestic economy of each nation will have distinct characteristics including such factors as population, per capita income, wage and salary levels, convertibility of currency, inflation rates, interest rates, and the system of taxation. In a second, broader context, the international manager must also take into account international economic factors. These

TABLE 2-1 The International Environment

Legal Environment	Cultural Environment
Legal tradition	Customs, norms, values, beliefs
Effectiveness of legal system	Language
Treaties with foreign nations	Attitudes
Patent trademark laws	Motivations
Laws affecting business firms	Social institutions
	Status symbols
	Religious beliefs

Economic Environment	Political System
Level of economic development	Form of government
Population	Political ideology
Gross national product	Stability of government
Per capita income	Strength of opposition parties and
Literacy level	groups
Social infrastructure	Social unrest
Natural resources	Political strife and insurgency
Climate	Governmental attitude towards
Membership in regional economic	foreign firms
blocks (EEC; LAFTA . . .)	Foreign policy
Monetary and fiscal policies	
Nature of competition	
Currency convertibility	
Inflation	
Taxation system	
Interest rates	
Wage and salary levels	

Source: Arvind V. Phatak, *International Dimensions of Management*, 2nd ed. (Boston: PWS-Kent Publishing Company, 1989), p. 6.

include economic indicators that are viewed from a more global perspective and are a result of trade and other interactions between nations.[2]

The *cultural* environment includes a host of variables that influence behavior and the manner in which the world is perceived. These may include such factors as language, attitudes, customs, value and belief systems, and religious affiliations. It is imperative that international managers have an understanding of different work habits and ways of living, and a general sensitivity to the cultural norms of the countries in which the firm does business. The impact of these factors on the success of international business operations cannot be overstated. Cross-cultural management takes into account the differences and similarities in people's behavior in organizations around the world. To be effective, training programs must be responsive to these differences. As organizations become more international in nature, managing employees from diverse cultures will pose significant challenges.[3] It is not surprising that among other predictions for the global 90s, human resource management is recognized as probably the most important factor in providing a competitive edge for both companies and countries.[4]

Political systems vary by country and may affect business management on an international scale. In fact, the *political* environment has been recognized as the major factor influencing international business decisions. Government negotiations and nationalism have been shown to be major problems for international management.[5] The firm may be affected by political conditions and issues in the country of operation and have little or no control over the course of events. Political instability and government takeovers can result in new regulations and leadership that are certain to place added hardships on the international manager.

The international *legal* environment of business is closely linked to the political domain. The political climate of business is reflected in the prevalent attitudes toward local and foreign business, how the country's laws are enforced, and the directions that new legislation takes.[6] Since there is currently no single, international legal system, the legal environment of business consists of the laws and regulations of the many nations of the world. It is important to have an understanding of the country's legal structure since these systems may vary considerably in philosophy and practice.[7]

Environmental influences will certainly be more pronounced in certain parts of the world. The significance of the four dimensions discussed in this section will vary by country. In some countries, for example, political constraints will be most prevalent, while in others, economic variables may have the greatest impact on business decision making.

A CONCEPTUAL MODEL LINKING THE IS FUNCTION WITH ITS INTERNATIONAL ENVIRONMENT

To facilitate our discussions, it will be useful to keep in mind a conceptual model that incorporates the environmental dimensions as they relate to the firm's IS function. This framework will provide a meaningful foundation from which to discuss environmental influences and identify important technological and managerial issues confronted by IS executives on a global scale. For these discussions, we will make use of a model developed by Deans and Ricks that addresses, in particular, the international dimensions specific to the MIS functional area of business.[8]

It will be helpful to first describe the development of this model in order to better understand the conceptual thought process that goes into defining the international dimensions of any business function. The basic foundation of the model is based on the Nolan and Wetherbe framework that defines a domain for the MIS field and is one of the few comprehensive models from the MIS literature that incorporates environmental variables.[9] The skeletal framework of the Nolan and Wetherbe model is presented in Figure 2–1. The purpose of this model is to show the eclectic characteristics of the MIS field modeled to represent the relationships between the MIS function, the organization of which it is a part, and the environment of the organization (for example, competitors, government, suppliers, customers). Note that the model identifies environmental influences in a general sense but does not distinguish variables specific to the international domain. This model can be modified

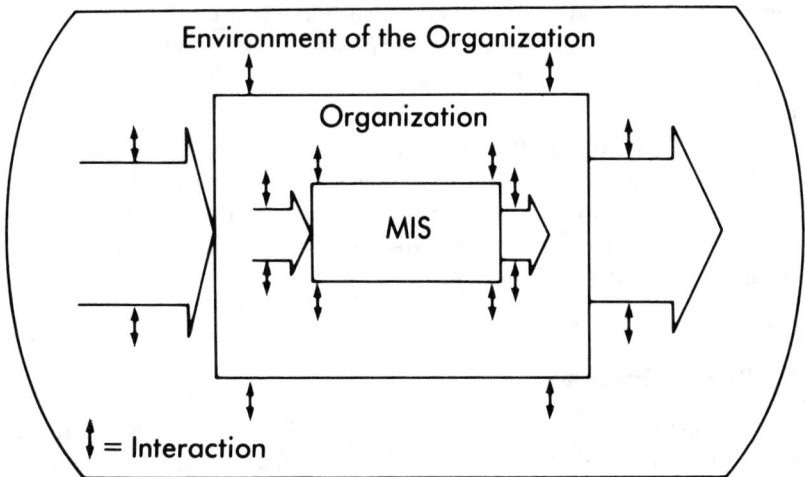

FIGURE 2–1   Overall Model of MIS and Its Environment

Source: Reprinted by special permission from the *MIS Quarterly*, vol. 4, no. 2, June 1980. Copyright 1980 by the Society for Information Management and the Management Information Systems Research Center at the University of Minnesota.

and extended in order to identify variables relevant to the firm's international business operating environment.

In order to define the international dimensions of the model, relevant frameworks and models from the international business literature are incorporated. Some modification of the previously discussed foreign dimensions for international management is necessary for the model to have maximum relevance for the IS function. In particular, a model proposed by Skinner that addresses international dimensions for the production function proves useful in the development of the IS model.[10] In his representation of environmental complexities, Skinner identified four interacting systems that are of particular concern for the international production manager: technological, cultural, political, and economic. The technological dimension that he added in the production context is, likewise, appropriate for addressing international IS issues.

The resulting framework presented in Figure 2–2 incorporates dimensions from both the Nolan and Wetherbe and Skinner models. As noted in the figure, the organization under consideration is the U.S.-based multinational corporation. The external environment has been broken down into domestic, international and foreign components. The technological dimension as utilized by Skinner is incorporated. The remaining dimensions of the foreign environment are identified as political/legal, social/cultural, and economic. This classification scheme is based on iterative interviews with IS executives in U.S.-based MNCs and depicts what is believed to be an appropriate model for the IS functional area.[11]

It will be helpful at this point to better define the dimensions of the model and, in particular, distinguish among the domestic, foreign, and international environments which the IS manager must address. These definitions are important in understanding the scope of international business and its relation to the firm's domestic business activity.

The Domestic Environment

The domestic environment represents those forces that are specific to the country in which the firm is based (referred to as the *home country*). As emphasized in Chapter 1, there are also economic, political, cultural, and legal dimensions specific to the firm's domestic environment. For the U.S.-based MNC, domestic environmental factors include variables such as economic indicators; governmental influence; and relationships with suppliers, customers, and competitors within the boundaries of the

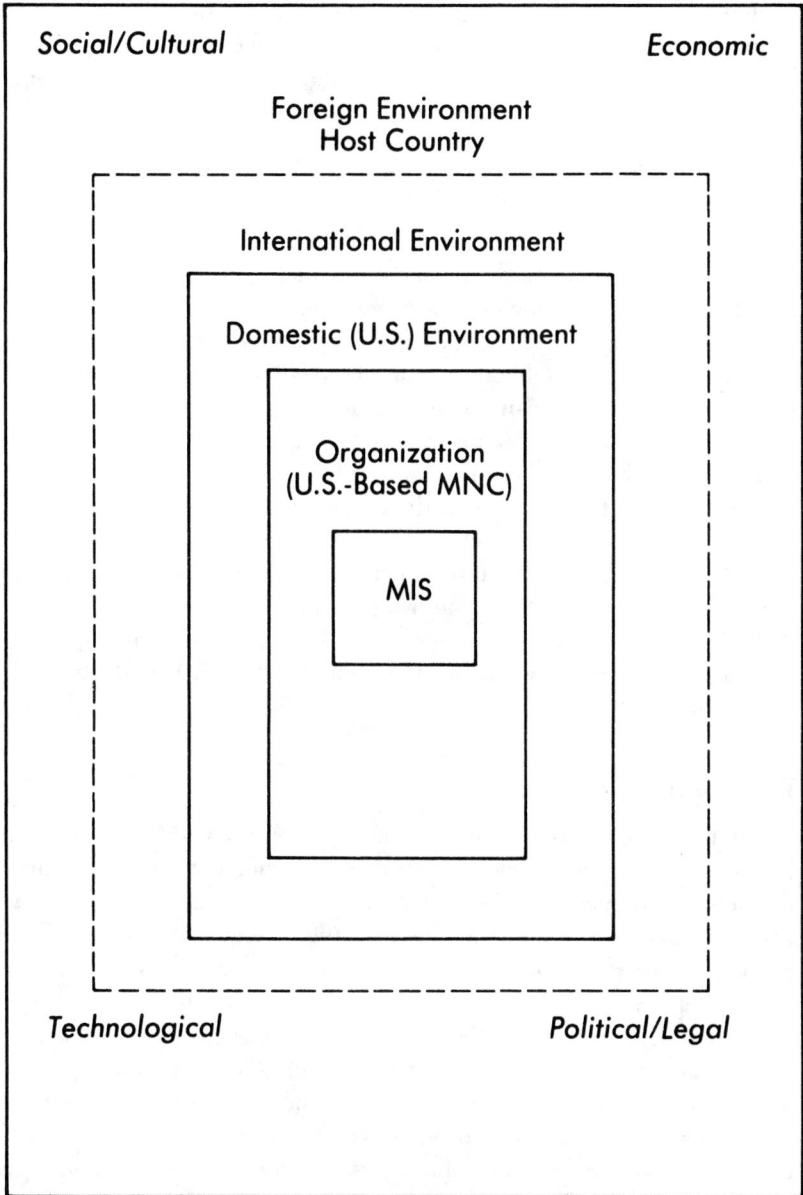

FIGURE 2-2   MIS/International Business Research Model

Source: P. Candace Deans and David A. Ricks, "MIS Research: A Model for Incorporating the International Dimension," *Journal of High Technology Management Research* (vol. 2, no. 1, Spring 1991).

United States. The IS manager has experience in dealing with these factors, which can be viewed from a more homogeneous perspective. For a foreign MNC, the domestic environment encompasses the same variables, but the variables are relevant to the country in which the MNC is based.

The Foreign Environment

The foreign environment is represented by the outer boundary of Figure 2–2 and encompasses the domestic operations within a foreign country. For the IS manager, the foreign environment represents the unique set of constraints and variables that must be dealt with in each country in which the firm does business. For example, Brazilian legislation designed to protect the local industry stipulates that hardware be purchased within Brazil. Each country has its own laws, regulations, and policies that are different from other countries and the United States. Each foreign market represents a unique challenge for the IS manager as integration of technologies and international standards for data transfer become increasingly important. Since our model is designed from the perspective of the U.S.-based MNC, the foreign dimension represents environmental factors for each country outside the United States in which the MNC has affiliates.

The International Environment

The international business environment is represented by the broken boundary line between the foreign-domestic and U.S.-domestic environments, and encompasses the interaction of environmental forces between the home country and those of the foreign nations where the company does business (host countries). Concerns and issues specific to the international dimension of the model represent interaction between the IS function, the organization of which it is a part, and the dimensions of the external environment—domestic, international, and foreign. International issues are viewed with a global orientation rather than from the perspective of unique attributes within foreign countries. International forces become significant as firms set up information systems that cross national boundaries. As the firm tries to coordinate its IS operations across diverse foreign environments, unique country constraints add further complexity to global integration.

Although this model focuses on environmental influences from the perspective of the U.S.-based MNC, it should again be noted that this model can be used for foreign multinational corporations as well. Our discussions here, however, will be directed toward those issues and concerns of particular relevance for MIS managers in U.S.-based MNCs.

THE IS FUNCTION WITHIN THE MULTINATIONAL CORPORATION

As noted by Cash, McFarlan, and McKenney, the IS function within the multinational corporation will be affected by company variables as well as country variables. Management of the IS function on a global scale inevitably takes place in an environment in which the relationships between these factors are complex.[12] As shown in Figure 2–2, it is first necessary to consider variables specific to the organization of which the IS function is a part. In the context of our discussions, that organization is the U.S.-based MNC.

From the perspective of the organization, Cash, McFarlan, and McKenney provide a discussion of many factors that may influence how the firm's information technology will be managed and controlled. First, the nature of the firm's business, whether service or manufacturing, and the firm's specific industry sector, play an important role in the development of the firm's information systems. For services, information is often a product in itself or is a part of the service the firm offers. Manufacturing firms, however, produce tangible goods and products. The international differences for service and manufacturing firms will be discussed in more detail in Chapter 3.

The role of the firm's IS activity and its importance to the organization may also determine the significance of international environmental variables. For some firms, the IS function necessarily plays a more strategic role, while for others it primarily represents a support infrastructure for the firm's business activity. Other variables such as the firm's international organizational structure may affect the level of IS coordination and support that is necessary. As the firm's international activity grows, it is typical for the firm to adopt appropriate management structures. Different structures will, out of necessity, require different levels of information technology support. The size of the company in absolute terms as well as its relative international involvement are also important considerations in determining the significance of international variables. International involvement may be measured in terms of foreign sales, foreign assets, foreign employees, foreign subsidiaries, or number of countries in which the firm does business. All these variables may play a significant part when considering the influence of environmental variables on the firm.

Ball and McCulloch define the environment as the sum of all forces influencing the life and development of the firm, and they categorize these forces as either external or internal.[13] The external forces are those over which management may exert some influence but has no direct control. Variables specific to the foreign environment, for example, would fall into this category. Internal forces are forces over which management has some control factors—such as production (capital, raw materials, and people) and organizational activities (finance, personnel, and production). Managers must address the controllable forces in order to react to changes in the uncontrollable variables. Organizational variables may, therefore, play a significant role in the degree of control and power the firm may exert in reacting to its international environmental influences.

INTERNATIONAL IS ISSUES

The model presented in the previous section provides one means by which to organize and discuss issues of significance to multinational IS executives. An empirical study reported by Deans, Karwan, Goslar, Ricks, and Toyne[14] identifies and ranks important international information systems issues for U.S.-based MNCs. The study results are based on a mail questionnaire and follow-up interviews with top IS executives in U.S.-based multinational corporations. Findings based on this work strongly support the contention that multinational IS managers encounter unique concerns as a result of operating in a global marketplace. A list of original issues, including neutral statements of explanation, is provided in Table 2–2. The ranked list, based on the study results, is presented in Table 2–3. It is important to note that this list of issues represents one set of concerns at a given point in time. It must also be stressed that international IS issues are linked to high levels of change and learning. Consequently, the issues and their significance will vary over time. We will use this particular set of issues to provide an overview of significant international IS concerns in the context of our model.

The international IS issues identified through the Deans et al. study can be incorporated into the existing model. This classification of issues depicted in Figure 2–3 is based on iterative interviews with IS executives and follow-up refinements.[15] Several interesting observations can be

TABLE 2-2 International Information Systems (IS) Issues

ALIGNING THE *IS* ORGANIZATION   The effectiveness with which IS can support international information needs may be affected by the position of IS within the overall organization of the MNC.

BANNED USAGE OF TELECOMMUNICATIONS EQUIPMENT   In some countries, certain types of telecommunications equipment may be banned.

CENTRALIZATION/DISTRIBUTED PROCESSING   There may be a need to balance the advantages and disadvantages of distributed versus centralized operations to take into account different country variables and restrictions.

CHANGES IN TELECOMMUNICATIONS TECHNOLOGY   Long-term international telecommunication decisions may need to be made despite continuing technological changes.

COMPUTER-INTEGRATED MANUFACTURING   Integration of factory systems with corporate information systems in the international context may warrant consideration.

CURRENCY RESTRICTIONS AND EXCHANGE RATE VOLATILITY   International data centers that are cost effective and competitive may suddenly become cost ineffective due to currency fluctuations.

DATA SECURITY   The balance between data security and data availability in the international domain can be complex.

DATA UTILIZATION   Data and technology should be managed so that information is accessible to the right people in a timely manner. It may be necessary to consider different time zones, holidays, working hours, and so on, in the international context.

EDUCATING SENIOR PERSONNEL   It may be important for corporate management to understand the role of MIS and its potential contribution on an international scale.

END-USER COMPUTING   Policy guidelines, communication, and support of end-user computing have become necessary, and the problems may be even more acute in the international environment.

EXPORT RESTRICTIONS   There may be restrictions on the export of data processing equipment and software to some countries.

EXTERNAL DATA   It may be important to heighten user awareness of data and databases external to the organization and their potential uses in an international context.

continued

TABLE 2-2, continued

INTEGRATED SERVICES DIGITAL NETWORK (ISDN)   The strategic implications of this technology and the potential impact on telecommunications may prompt corporations to become advised and aware of developments in its use and applications.

INTEGRATION OF TECHNOLOGIES   It may be necessary to integrate data processing, telecommunications, and automated office technologies on an international scale.

INTERNATIONAL MIS PLANNING   MIS planning may be more difficult due to rapidly changing technology—especially in the context of complex multinational information systems.

INTERNATIONAL PROTOCOL STANDARDS   There may be a need for standardized information exchange, for example, Electronic Data Interchange (EDI) or Trade Data Interchange (TDI). Network standards supporting open communications architecture and connectivity among vendor products may be important issues.

INTERORGANIZATIONAL SYSTEMS   The sharing of information systems among companies may be of concern for MNCs.

LANGUAGE BARRIERS   Technical communications, documentation, and communication among personnel may be hindered by the lack of a common language.

LEARNING TO CONDUCT IS BUSINESS IN OTHER COUNTRIES   It may be necessary to become aware of the potential difficulties that can be encountered when operating in other countries.

LEGAL RESTRICTIONS ON HARDWARE/SOFTWARE ACQUISITION   In order to protect their data and information processing industries, some countries may require that hardware and software be purchased locally.

LEVEL OF INFORMATION TECHNOLOGY (IT) SOPHISTICATION IN THE COUNTRY   The speed and ease for implementing an IT activity may depend on conditions that already exist with respect to installed information systems.

LOCAL CULTURAL CONSTRAINTS   A network of cultural facets may make the development of coordinated systems and the transfer of technology difficult. Union agreements and customs procedures, for example, may force software modification tailored to local languages and ease of use.

PRICE AND QUALITY OF TELECOMMUNICATIONS
Communication quality, availability, and cost may differ widely from one country to another. Lead times for lines may be long, if available at all.

TABLE 2-2, continued

RECRUITING AND TRAINING   Shortages of qualified personnel, especially in some countries, may increase the importance of recruiting and training.

REGULATORY STRATEGIES OF PTTs   In many countries, postal, telegraph and telephone (PTT) monopolies may regulate MNCs and provide obstacles to a cost-effective transfer of data.

SOFTWARE DEVELOPMENT   Quality, faster development, and standardization of software may be important. Many country variables such as different legal and accounting systems may affect software development in the international context.

TELECOMMUNICATIONS DEREGULATION   Due to concerns about deregulation, quality assurance of telecommunications operations may be important in the international environment.

THE NATIONAL INFRASTRUCTURE   The availability of a transportation system and utilities in some countries may constrain feasible technology alternatives.

TRANSBORDER DATA FLOW RESTRICTIONS   Legal restrictions on the transfer of data in some countries may pose obstacles for multinational corporations and heighten concern as to future developments.

USE OF INFORMATION TECHNOLOGY FOR COMPETITIVE ADVANTAGE   Some corporations claim to be successfully using information systems technology for competitive advantage. It may become necessary to be aware of the possibilities and implications for the MNC's international operations.

USE OF VALUE-ADDED NETWORK SERVICES (VANS) BY MNCs   VANS offer electronic mail, trade data interchange, electronic document distribution, remote computing, remote database applications, and so on, internationally within the same enterprise and among different enterprises.

VENDOR SUPPORT IN FOREIGN SUBSIDIARIES   The size of the local market may influence the number of vendors as well as the quality of vendor support.

Source: P. Candace Deans, Kirk R. Karwan, Martin D. Goslar, David A. Ricks, and Brian Toyne, "Identification of Key International Information Systems Issues in U.S.-Based Multinational Corporations," *Journal of Management Information Systems* (vol. 7, no. 4, Spring 1991).

TABLE 2-3   Rank in Means of Issues for All Respondents

Rank	Issue	Mean	Standard Deviation
1.	Educating senior personnel	5.331	1.3831
2.	Data security	5.231	1.4549
3.	Integration of technologies	5.225	1.5574
4.	End-user computing	5.208	1.3393
5.	Price and quality of telecommunications	5.208	1.4451
6.	International protocol standards	5.177	1.4222
7.	Use of information technology for competitive advantage	5.169	1.4581
8.	Data utilization	5.085	1.5801
9.	Telecommunications deregulation	4.908	1.3890
10.	Changes in telecommunications technology	4.769	1.3840
11.	Aligning the IS organization	4.677	1.4691
12.	Centralization/distributed processing	4.662	1.5478
13.	Recruiting and training	4.608	1.3497
14.	Software development	4.585	1.5391
15.	Regulatory strategies of PTTs	4.562	1.6844
16.	Integrated services digital network (ISDN)	4.554	1.5100
17.	Learning to conduct IS business in other countries	4.535	1.7457

noted about the model. First, many of the original thirty-two issues may be classified as country-specific issues unique to the countries or foreign environments in which the corporation operates. Other issues are viewed as representing interaction between the MIS function; the organization; and its domestic, international, and foreign environments. Those issues recognized as posing problems internationally but not having unique attributes within countries will be referred to as *international* while the remaining issues are identified as *country-specific* issues.

The issues identified as international in scope are further classified as either management/enterprise-related or technology/application-oriented. This categorization is based on a similar scheme utilized by

TABLE 2-3, continued

Rank	Issue	Mean	Standard Deviation
18.	International MIS planning	4.512	1.7371
19.	Vendor support in foreign subsidiaries	4.385	1.6396
20.	Use of value added networks (VANs) by MNCs	4.180	1.5340
21.	External data	4.177	1.3722
22.	Local cultural constraints	4.177	1.6447
23.	Transborder data flow restrictions	4.146	1.8177
24.	Legal restrictions on software/hardware acquisition	4.138	1.6460
25.	Level of information technology sophistication in the country	4.132	1.5072
26.	Interorganizational systems	3.962	1.5770
27.	Banned usage of telecommunications equipment	3.938	1.7242
28.	Language barriers	3.846	1.6911
29.	The national infrastructure	3.800	1.6349
30.	Computer-integrated manufacturing	3.631	1.8263
31.	Currency restrictions and exchange rate volatility	3.623	1.5059
32.	Export restrictions	3.462	1.5559

Note: Ties in rankings of issues are represented by the same number.

Source: P. Candace Deans, Kirk R. Karwan, Martin D. Goslar, David A. Ricks, and Brian Toyne, "Identification of Key International Information Systems Issues in U.S.-Based Multinational Corporations," *Journal of Management Information Systems* (vol. 7, no. 4, Spring 1991).

Brancheau and Wetherbe in their 1987 study of domestic IS issues.[16] Based exclusively on numbers, the list of thirty-two IS issues under consideration is dominated by these technological and managerial concerns. As might be expected, many of these broad concerns are important for both the international and domestic IS arenas. It should be recognized that many of the issues identified here have both technological and managerial dimensions. These categorizations are based on what is perceived to be the dominant emphasis. The issues categorized as international represent those issues that are more controllable. A majority of the top priority issues fall within this dimension (see Table 2–3). Country-specific issues, on the other hand, generally represent constraints or areas

Social/Cultural
Cultural constraints
Language

Economic
Export restrictions
Currency restrictions and
    exchange rate volatility
The national infrastructure

Foreign Environment
Host Country

International Environment

Domestic (U.S.) Environment

Organization
(U.S.-Based MNC)

MIS

*Technological/Application
Data security
Data utilization
Software development
Integration of technologies
International protocol standards
Use of value added networks
Computer integrated manufacturing
Integrated services digital networks
Changes in telecommunications technology

*Managerial/Strategic
Educating senior personnel
End-user computing
Use of information technology for
    competitive advantage
International MIS planning
Aligning the *IS* organization
Centralization/distributed processing
Learning to conduct IS business
    in other countries
Interorganizational systems
External data
Recruiting and training

Technological
Regulatory strategies of the PTTs
Vendor support in foreign subsidiaries
Level of information technology sophistication
    in the country
Price and quality of telecommunications

Political/Legal
Transborder data flow restrictions
Legal restrictions on
    hardware/software acquisition
Telecommunications deregulation
Banned usage of telecommunications
    equipment

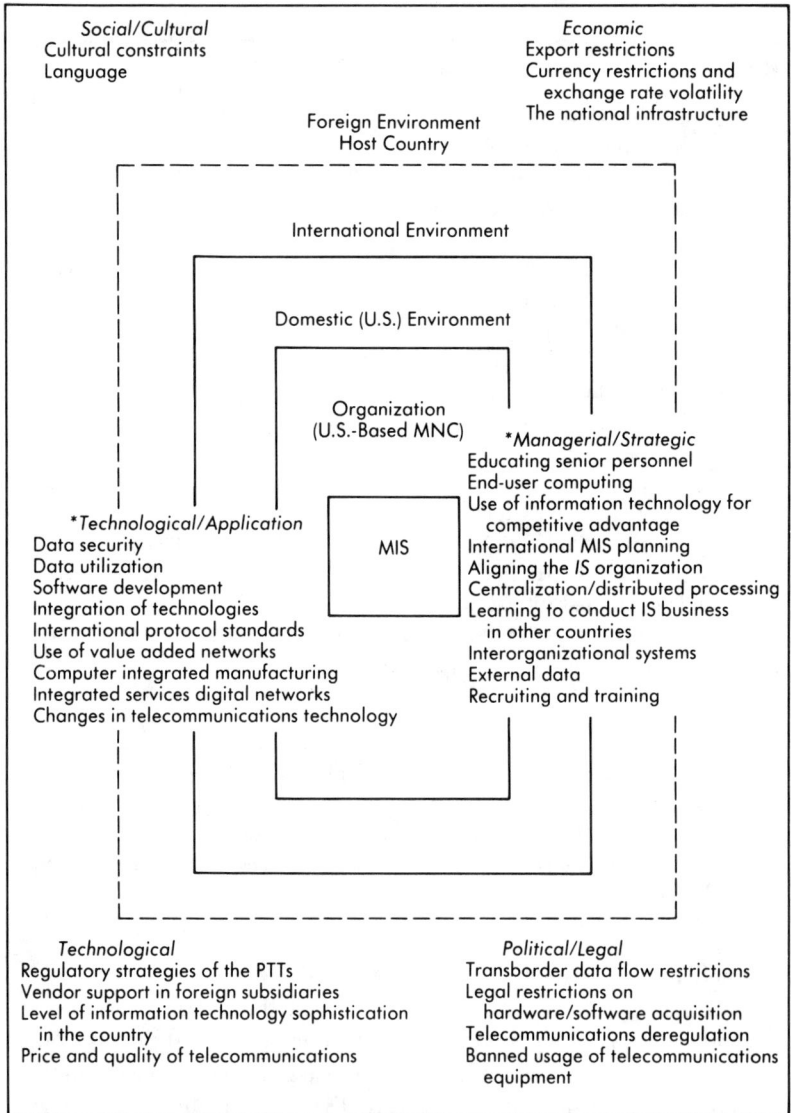

*These issues entail varying interactions between the corporate IS function, the strategy and
policies of the MNC, and the international, foreign, and domestic environments.

FIGURE 2 – 3   MIS/International Business Issue Categorization

Source: P. Candace Deans and David A. Ricks, "MIS Research: A Model for Incorporating the International Dimension," *Journal of High Technology Management Research* (vol. 2, no. 1, Spring 1991).

that are less controllable. As shown in Table 2–3, these issues are not rated as highly in importance as issues that are more controllable.[17]

THE COUNTRY-SPECIFIC ISSUES

There are many significant issues that are unique to the country of operation. The country-specific issues identified in Figure 2–3 represent a set of constraints relevant to the IS function. These issues are broad based and encompass many specific components. For example, different accounting and legal systems, work ethics, reporting requirements, and timing of holidays and work hours are only a few of the concerns that may complicate the firm's data-gathering and reporting processes outside the United States. This list of country-specific issues should not be thought of as exhaustive or static. The dynamic nature of this process cannot be overstated.

As shown in Figure 2–3, many of the country-specific issues fall within either the technological or political/legal dimensions of the foreign component of the model. These issues focus on concerns relevant to the firm's international telecommunications. A more in-depth discussion of these issues will be provided in Chapter 5. As noted in Table 2–3, these issues are generally of greater concern than social/cultural and economic issues are to international IS executives.

Although the issues listed in Table 2–3 that are related to each of the four foreign dimensions are not generally top priority in this broad context, the importance of specific issues depends on many factors. There may be interactions among factors affecting the four environments that will affect the rank of these issues. For example, government take-over in a given country may result in changes in postal, telephone, and telegraph (PTT) regulations. Although most of the country-specific issues are of lower importance, it is clear that IS managers must monitor them and be concerned with the uncontrollable environment in which they operate.[18]

Particular dimensions of the foreign environment are more important for certain functional areas. For example, in the international marketing area, the economic and social/cultural dimensions are important in determining marketing behavior. For international finance, the economic environment is of particular importance.[19]

The same is also true of the MIS area. IS managers do not view the four dimensions of the foreign environment as imposing a uniform set of constraints. For example, they see the technological dimension as being more important than the other three because this dimension directly affects international telecommunications. This is not surprising since IS decisions often focus on technological concerns and the IS executive has always been involved heavily with technology (as opposed to economic, social/cultural, and legal/political concerns). Issues identified with the political/legal environment are also of general concern although this is not as apparent from their relative mean scores. Issues specific to the social/cultural and economic environments are, however, uniformly identified as being of lower priority. Issues in these dimensions are of concern, but IS managers tend to view these as issues that are less controllable and in which they have very little influence. Executives in larger MNCs have confronted these issues for years and are more experienced in dealing with these problems. Although these issues are comparatively important, they are not as significant to the IS executive.[20]

Evidence clearly indicates that difficulties associated with international IS go beyond those associated with distance alone. Country-specific variables unique to the political/legal environment, the economic environment, the social/cultural environment, and the technological environment of the MIS functional area have been identified. These issues are clearly specific to the foreign environment rather than a function of the distance involved.[21]

THE TECHNOLOGICAL ISSUES

From a technological perspective, several issues are recognized as posing particular problems for the management of data and information exchange and the establishment of communication networks across national boundaries. Technological concerns, whether categorized as country-specific or international in scope, tend to dominate the list of issues presented in Table 2-3. Two general areas drawing significant attention include issues relevant to the transfer of data and information across national borders and issues specific to the firm's international telecommunications function. These two topics will be addressed in chapters 4 and 5. Only an overview of the important dimensions will be presented here.

International Transfer of Data and Information

Many relevant issues contribute to obstacles that MNCs may encounter as they transfer information and share data with foreign subsidiary operations. Legal restrictions on the transfer of data and information from one country to another may pose problems in some countries. International standards for the transfer of data across national borders may impede the cost-effectiveness and timeliness of information transfer. Regulations imposed by bodies such as the postal, telephone, and telegraph companies may also further complicate these processes. The significance of these issues will likely change over time as data traffic and information transfers continue to increase and play a more important part in the firm's international operations.

International Telecommunications

Currently, MNCs may encounter many obstacles as they strive for global connectivity. The existing national infrastructure for telecommunications has tremendous implications when establishing communication links between foreign affiliates and headquarter operations. The availability of options may limit possible alternatives. The quality and cost of telecommunications, telecommunications regulations, vendor support in foreign countries, and international standards add further complexities to the design and management of the firm's information systems. Data security concerns become more complex as the need to integrate existing technologies on a global scale becomes even more pressing. These concerns are becoming increasingly significant as businesses put pressure on standards organizations and political groups to respond to their needs.

THE MANAGERIAL ISSUES

International managerial concerns are more difficult to articulate and present particular challenges for a constantly changing technological world. It has become increasingly important for firms to develop a technological infrastructure that can easily accommodate change. IS executives in MNCs with greater foreign involvement tend to have more international experience in general as well as more experience with the technology and, therefore, they tend to place greater significance on managerial concerns. The two broad areas of focus include issues specific to planning for international information systems and the strategic implications of information technology. These two topics will be discussed at greater length in chapters 6 and 7.

Planning for International IS

Planning for information systems has become an especially complex task domestically and is further complicated internationally by the many constraints and variations imposed by different operating environments.

As expected, those firms with greater international involvement place greater emphasis on the importance of this issue. Many larger MNCs have set up separate departments for international information systems. Planning for the firm's information systems requires corporate-level support and understanding of the issues involved. As shown in Table 2–3, *Educating senior personnel* received top-priority concern among IS executives. Senior management needs to have a better appreciation of the problems and opportunities that information technology may bring to the firm on an international scale. It cannot be assumed that what works in the United States will work anywhere else in the world.

IS executives believe that the communication gap between senior management and IS management will narrow with the changing mixture of senior executives and as newer people who have grown up with the IS issues take over management positions. Executives see further changes occurring as the corporation becomes more competitive internationally, as deregulation and a keener interest in the organization evolve, and as IS becomes a major expense component.

International planning for IS is a complicated task and is linked to other international IS concerns. Systems planning involves coordination with other dimensions of the organization. Human resource management, for example, is linked to IS planning. In particular, recruiting and training personnel will influence the sophistication of systems that are appropriate for a given country. Planning for the end-user computing environment has become an increasingly important concern, especially in an international context. Decisions about centralizing or decentralizing the firm's data processing operations internationally are also directly linked to the firm's overall IS plan.

Strategic Implications of IT

Information technology is increasingly being recognized as a viable competitive weapon with potential strategic significance for the firm. *Use of IT for competitive advantage* is recognized as one of the top priority issues for international IS. Specific to the firm's international business operations, the following areas are among those that have strategic implications:

1. Cooperation in the form of joint ventures and partnerships with foreign companies to aid in the use of IT for competitive advantage.

2. Implementation of specific technologies such as teleconferencing (to replace travel), video teleconferencing (to provide interactive training in geographically distant locations), facsimile (in lieu of the postal system), and electronic mail (in lieu of phone calls). Use of these technologies may prove to be more cost effective and may avoid time zone differences and language barriers.

3. Use of IT to support new organizational structures (for example, matrix management) and provide better means for managing across functions, business units, product markets, and geographic units.

4. Use of more powerful workstations and advancements in PC technology with more emphasis on the end user.

IS executives tend to agree on three goals that are most important for their international IS: to share information worldwide and quickly, to shrink geographic boundaries and time barriers, and to integrate technologies with clear directions and products. Several executives stressed the need for worldwide, compatible telecommunication links and standards to provide the means for quick, fast movement of data in the global economy. There are, of course, many environmental forces that will require understanding and compromise.

SUMMARY

An array of international environmental factors must be considered as the firm increases its international business activity and involvement. From the perspective of the firm's IS function, factors must be evaluated that are specific to the organization as well as the domestic, international, and foreign environments in which the firm participates. The domestic environment encompasses those factors relevant to the home country in which the firm resides. The foreign environment(s) represent(s) the unique set of constraints and characteristics that must be considered in each country in which the firm does business. The international operating environment comprises the interaction of forces between the domestic and foreign environments. There are many interacting factors in an integrated world economy that will affect decision making and add further complexity to the task of global integration. The IS function will play an important part as the firm's central link in this evolving global environment.

The framework presented in Figure 2–2 represents one classification scheme for identifying issues relevant to the controllable and uncontrollable environments in which the multinational corporation operates. The framework further identifies a means by which multinational IS managers can begin to understand the major forces in the technological, social/cultural, legal/political, and economic dimensions of the foreign environments in which they do business. As emphasized by Skinner, it is important to recognize demands imposed by these environmental forces on managerial decision making. Executives must learn to recognize those factors that are *fixed*, those that are *changeable*, and those that are *most critical* in each of these dimensions. They can then focus their attention on those factors over which they have some control or influence.[22] IS management with international responsibilities currently faces a dynamic internal environment. The forces from the domestic, international, and foreign environments contribute further complexity to an intricate decision-making process. In the following chapters, many of the issues introduced here will be discussed in greater depth.

NOTES

1. Arvind V. Phatak, *International Dimensions of Management*, 2nd ed. (Massachusetts: PWS-Kent Publishing Co., 1989), 3.

2. Vern Terpstra, *International Marketing*, 3rd ed. (New York: The Dryden Press, 1983), 22.

3. Nancy J. Adler, *International Dimensions of Organizational Behavior* (Massachusetts: PWS-Kent Publishing Co., 1986), 4–5.

4. John Nasbitt and Patricia Aburdene, *Ten New Directions for the 1990s Megatrends 2000* (New York: William Morrow & Company, Inc., 1990), 39.

5. Terpstra, 119.

6. Ibid., 128.

7. Michael Litka, *International Dimensions of the Legal Environment of Business* (Massachusetts: PWS-Kent Publishing Company, 1988), 3.

8. P. Candace Deans and David A. Ricks, "MIS Research: A Model for Incorporating the International Dimension," *Journal of High Technology Management Research* (vol. 2, no. 1, 1991): 57–81.

9. R. L. Nolan and J. C. Wetherbe, "Toward a Comprehensive Framework for MIS Research," *MIS Quarterly* (June 1980): 1–19.

10. W. C. Skinner, "Management of International Production," *Harvard Business Review* (September–October 1964): 125–136.

11. Deans and Ricks, 74.

12. James I. Cash, Jr., Warren F. McFarlan, and James L. McKenney, *Corporate Information Systems Management* (Illinois: Richard D. Irwin, 1988), 219–223.

13. Donald A. Ball and Wendell H. McCulloch, *International Business* (Texas: Business Publications, 1985), 11.

14. P. Candace Deans, Kirk R. Karwan, Martin D. Goslar, David A. Ricks, and Brian Toyne, "Identification of Key International Information Systems Issues in U.S.-Based Multinational Corporations." *Journal of Management Information Systems* (vol. 7, no. 4, Spring 1991).

15. Deans and Ricks, 66.

16. James Brancheau and James Wetherbe, "Key Issues in Information Systems Management," *MIS Quarterly* (March 1987): 23–45.

17. Deans and Ricks, 72.

18. Ibid.

19. Ibid.

20. Ibid.

21. Ibid., 73.

22. Skinner, 131.

STUDY QUESTIONS

1. Assume the role of vice-president of international information systems in a large U.S.-based multinational corporation. Describe the foreign, international, and domestic environments in which the multinational MIS manager must operate.

2. How do the four components of the foreign environment influence the decision-making process of the MIS manager?

3. How is the IS function within the MNC different from a comparable domestic firm with little or no international involvement?

4. What is meant by a *country-specific* issue? Give an example and explain why this issue could be classified as country-specific.

5. Give examples of several international *technological* IS issues of significance to MIS executives.

6. Give examples of several international *managerial* IS issues of significance to MIS executives.

SUGGESTED READINGS

Adler, Nancy. "A Typology of Management Studies Involving Culture." *Journal of International Business Studies* (Fall 1983): 29–47.

Czinkota, Michael, Pietra Rivoli, and Ilka Ronkainen. *International Business*, Chicago: Dryden Press, 1989.

Daniels, John, and Lee Radebaugh. *International Business: Environments and Operations*, 4th ed. Reading, MA: Addison-Wesley, 1986.

Fagre, Nathan, and L. Wells. "Bargaining Power of Multinationals and Host Governments," *Journal of International Business Studies* (Fall 1982): 9–23.

Fayerweather, John. *International Business Strategy and Administration.* Cambridge, MA: Ballinger, 1982.

Ferraro, Gary P. *The Cultural Dimension of International Business.* New Jersey: Prentice Hall, 1990.

Grosse, Robert, and Duane Kujawa. *International Business: Theory and Managerial Applications.* Homewood, IL: Irwin, 1988.

Grub, Philip, F. Ghadar, and D. Khambata, eds. *The Multinational Enterprise in Transition*, 2nd ed. Princeton, NJ: Darwin Press, 1984.

Hall, Edward T. *The Silent Language.* New York: Doubleday, 1959.

Hall, Edward T. *Beyond Culture.* New York: Anchor Press/Doubleday, 1976.

Harris, R., and R. Moran. *Managing Cultural Differences*, 2nd ed. Houston: Gulf Publishing, 1987.

Kolde, Endel-Jakob. *Environment of International Business.* Boston: Kent Publishing Co., 1982.

Negandhi, Anant. *International Management.* Newton, MA: Allyn and Bacon, 1987.

Porter, Michael E. *The Competitive Advantage of Nations.* New York: Free Press, 1990.

Poynter, Thomas. "Managing Government Intervention: A Strategy for Defending the Subsidiary." *Columbia Journal of World Business* (Winter 1986): 58.

Punnett, Betty J. and David A. Ricks. *International Business.* Boston: PWS-Kent Publishing, 1992.

Robock, Stefan, and Kenneth Simmonds. *International Business and Multinational Enterprises*, 4th ed. Homewood, IL: Irwin, 1989.

Ronen, Simcha. *Comparative and International Management.* New York: Wiley, 1986.

Sugiura, Hideo. "How Honda Localizes Its Global Strategy." *Sloan Management Review* (Fall 1990): 77–82.

Terpstra, Vern, and Kenneth David. *The Cultural Environment of International Business*, 3rd ed. Ohio: South-Western Publishing Company, 1991.

Ting, Wenlee, *Multinational Risk Assessment and Management*. Westport, CT: Greenwood Press, 1988.

Vernon, Raymond, and Louis T. Wells, Jr. *The Manager in the International Economy*, 6th ed. New Jersey: Prentice Hall, 1991.

————. *The Economic Environment of International Business*, 4th ed. New Jersey: Prentice Hall, 1986.

Watson, Richard T., and James C. Brancheau. "Key Issues in Information Systems Management: An International Perspective." *Information and Management* (Spring 1991): 213–223.

Chapter THREE

A Closer Look at International Influences on IS Function: Service MNCs versus Manufacturing MNCs

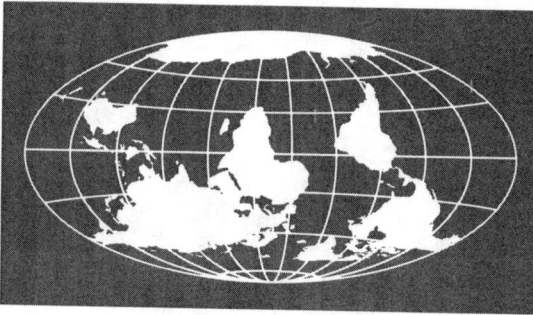

Over the past decade we have experienced a pronounced change in the American economy from one based on industry to one based on service and information. During this century we have moved from an economy with a power base in land and most of the work force employed by the agricultural sector to an industrial economy in which the power shifted to capital and an industrial workforce and, finally, to an information economy in which power now lies in information and the work force is dominated by knowledge workers of a service economy.[1]

According to Peter Drucker, we are fast moving from the typical manufacturing company to an organization that more closely resembles the service firm.[2] Many factors are contributing to this shift, including demographics, economics, and the move from clerical workers to knowledge workers. Drucker stresses that, above all, information technology demands the shift.[3] Based on a comprehensive study of curriculum trends in business schools, Porter and McKibbin conclude that the change from an economy based on industry to one based on service and information will likely be the most significant of all variables affecting the future environment for which business leaders will need to be prepared.[4]

Services are becoming an increasingly important component of the U.S. economy. The service sector produces well over half of the nation's GNP and employs over 80 percent of the workforce.[5] These trends have put the United States in the position of being a net services exporter. Internationally, similar changes are taking place as the world market for services is growing at a rate twice that of product trade.[6] The marketing of services is becoming a significant component of world business. It is predicted that by the year 2000, more than half of all multinational firms will be service corporations.[7]

Although a continuum usually exists from pure service to pure manufacturing, the nature of the business activity of service firms is different from that of manufacturing firms. From an information systems perspective, the firm's needs and information requirements may differ, and it has become necessary to look more closely at these differences. In this chapter we will examine the international IS issues identified in Chapter 2 in terms of differences and similarities for service firms and manufacturing firms. We will also discuss implications for a number of other international organizational variables in the context of these service and manufacturing differences.

MULTINATIONAL SERVICE VERSUS MANUFACTURING

A number of unique characteristics distinguish service from manufacturing (including intangibility, inseparability of production and consumption, heterogeneity, and perishability).[8] It has been argued that intangibility is the critical distinction from which all other differences emerge.[9] From the perspective of the multinational firm, these same differences are recognized for manufacturing and for service. The nature of foreign investment is different for service MNCs than for manufacturing firms because services are usually less capital intensive, and a major motive for going abroad is to service home country clients in foreign countries.[10] Multinational services are currently receiving increased attention. Given the anticipated growth in service multinationals, practitioners and academicians will likely continue to be interested in the service sector.

A key finding of the Deans et al. study discussed in the previous chapter reveals that the importance of international IS issue ratings vary (that is, in a statistical sense) for U.S.-based service and manufacturing MNCs. This result suggests that the concerns facing multinational services may be somewhat different from those confronting manufacturing MNCs.[11] The business activity of service firms is more directly involved in processing data and information, whereas manufacturing firms place more emphasis on production of tangible goods. Even though this distinction is narrowing, information systems needs vary according to the nature of the firm's primary business activity. It should be noted that the distinction made here between service and manufacturing is based on the definition used by the Fortune Industrial and Service 500s.

Results of the international IS issues study also imply that many other variables relating to the configuration of international business operations (for example, number of foreign subsidiaries, firm size, location of foreign subsidiaries, and level of international involvement) may contribute to the difference between service and manufacturing MNCs. Although additional research is necessary to more specifically substantiate these influences, possible implications of these variables will be discussed in this chapter.

THE INTERNATIONAL ISSUES: SERVICE VERSUS MANUFACTURING

The international IS issues identified and discussed in Chapter 2 can now be compared from the perspectives of the multinational service and manufacturing firms. Although the top priority issues are similar, the ordering of the issues varies by firm type. To highlight these differences and aid in our discussions, Table 3–1 provides a comparison of issue mean scores for both service and manufacturing firms. As alluded to previously, statistical results indicate a difference for service and manufacturing firms in terms of the overall importance of the issues.[12]

Further statistical evaluation of the differences reveals seven issues that account most for the overall difference. These issues are depicted

TABLE 3-1 Comparison of Means for Service/Manufacturing

Rank	*Rank in Means of Issues for Service Corporations* Issue	Mean	Rank	*Rank in Means of Issues for Manufacturing Corporations* Issue	Mean
* 1.	Data security	5.5179	1.	Educating senior personnel	5.4154
* 2.	Data utilization	5.4107	2.	International protocol standards	5.3538
3.	Price and quality of telecommunications	5.3392	3.	Integration of technologies	5.2500
4.	End-user computing	5.2679	4.	Use of information technology (IT) for competitive advantage	5.1538
5.	Educating senior personnel	5.2143	5.	End-user computing	5.1231
6.	Integration of technologies	5.1786	6.	Price and quality of telecommunications technology	5.0615
7.	Use of information technology for competitive advantage	5.1607	* 7.	Data security	4.8769
8.	Telecommunications deregulation	5.0535	8.	Centralization/distributed processing	4.8615
9.	International protocol standards	4.9821	* 9.	Regulatory strategies of PTTs	4.8462
10.	Changes in telecommunications technology	4.7857	10.	Aligning the IS organization	4.7846
11.	Integrated services digital networks (ISDNs)	4.6786	11.	Telecommunications deregulation	4.7846
12.	Recruiting and training	4.5892	*12.	Data utilization	4.7230
13.	Aligning the IS organization	4.4642	13.	International MIS planning	4.7188
14.	International MIS planning	4.4286	14.	Changes in telecommunications technology	4.7077
15.	Software development	4.4286	*15.	Vendor support in foreign subsidiaries	4.6769
16.	Centralization/distributed processing	4.3928	16.	Software development	4.6615
17.	Learning to conduct IS business in other countries	4.3751	17.	Recruiting and training	4.6308
*18.	Regulatory strategies of PTTs	4.2143	*18.	Local cultural constraints	4.6308
19.	External data	4.1250	19.	Learning to conduct IS business in other countries	4.6250
*20.	Vendor support in foreign subsidiaries	4.0893			continued

TABLE 3–1, continued

	Rank in Means of Issues for Service Corporations		Rank in Means of Issues for Manufacturing Corporations	
21.	Use of value-added networks (VANs) by MNCs	4.0536	*20. Computer-integrated manufacturing	4.5231
22.	Transborder data flow restrictions	3.9821	21. Integrated services digital networks (ISDNs)	4.4308
*23.	Currency restrictions and exchange rate volatility	3.9464	22. Level of information technology sophistication in the country	4.3438
24.	Legal restrictions on hardware/software acquisition	3.9286	23. Use of value added networks (VANS) for MNCs	4.2381
25.	Level of information technology sophistication in the country	3.8929	24. Transborder data flow restrictions	4.2154
26.	Interorganizational systems	3.8393	25. Legal restrictions on hardware/software acquisition	4.1692
27.	Language barriers	3.8036	26. External data	4.1231
28.	The national infrastructure	3.7142	27. Banned usage of telecommunications equipment	4.0769
*29.	Local cultural constraints	3.6786	28. Interorganizational systems	3.9846
30.	Banned usage of telecommunications equipment	3.6250	29. Language barriers	3.8923
31.	Export restrictions	3.1250	30. The national infrastructure	3.8154
*32.	Computer-integrated manufacturing	2.5357	31. Export restrictions	3.6462
			*32. Currency restrictions and exchange rate volatility	3.3846

*These issues represent a statistically significant difference in response for manufacturing and service MNCs.

Source: P. Candace Deans, *The Transfer and Management of Information Systems (IS) Technology in the International Environment: Identification of Key Issues for MIS Managers in U.S.-Based Multinational Corporations*, Ph.D. Dissertation, University of South Carolina, 1989.

in Table 3–2 and include: *Computer-integrated manufacturing, Currency restrictions and exchange rate volatility, Vendor support in foreign subsidiaries, Local cultural constraints, Regulatory strategies of the PTTs, Data security*, and *Data utilization*. These seven issues are highlighted with asterisks in Table 3–1 to more clearly distinguish issues more important for services from issues more important for manufacturing firms.

It is not surprising that *Computer-integrated manufacturing* is a more important issue for manufacturing firms. Likewise, it is not unexpected that *Currency restrictions and exchange rate volatility* would be more important for service firms. Differences in business activity for service versus manufacturing firms account to a large degree for these findings. Explanations of differences for the other issues are more difficult to explain directly. These issues will be discussed in the following paragraphs with reference to interviews conducted with multinational IS executives.[13] Our discussion here will focus only on the perceived reasons for differences in the importance of these issues for service and manufacturing firms. The specific issues will be discussed in greater detail in later chapters.

In particular, interview results suggest that *Vendor support in foreign subsidiaries* is of greater concern for manufacturing firms since multinational manufacturing firms are more likely to implement decentralized data processing systems and service firms tend toward centralized systems. Service firms service their own IS operations from their domestic

TABLE 3–2   Major Issues of Difference for Service Firms versus Manufacturing Firms

Issues
Computer-integrated manufacturing
Currency restrictions and exchange rate volatility
Vendor support in foreign subsidiaries
Regulatory strategies of the PTTs
Local cultural constraints
Data security
Data utilization

Source: P. Candace Deans, Kirk R. Karwan, Martin D. Goslar, David A. Ricks, and Brian Toyne, "Identification of Key International Information Systems Issues in U.S.-Based Multinational Corporations," *Journal of Management Information Systems* (vol. 7, no. 4, Spring 1991).

headquarters, while manufacturing firms must necessarily rely on local vendors. Also, manufacturing firms tend to operate in more countries than service firms do, and vendor support varies from country to country. Service firms are more likely to use major vendors worldwide and, thus, not encounter as many problems. IS executives in service firms stressed a preference to operate only in countries where major vendors such as IBM and AT&T are present.

Manufacturing firms, in general, expressed concern about *Regulatory Strategies of PTTs* and rated this issue more highly than service firms rated it. Service firm executives gave several reasons for their relatively lower mean scores. Services tend to process information within the United States, have less equipment, and have limited international involvement. Some service firms indicated that they operate only in countries in which the PTTs are not known to cause particular problems. Another explanation for the relatively lower mean score for services is that service firms with limited international involvement may not be at a level to appreciate the concerns.

Local cultural constraints also surfaced as an issue of greater significance to manufacturing firms than service firms. The explanation for this finding, likewise, centered on the fact that manufacturing firms tend toward decentralized systems, which allow for more local authority and, consequently, more dependence on that country's culture. Manufacturing firms also tend to deal more with blue-collar workers and foreign unions, and are more likely to hire a high percentage of illiterate workers. In contrast, service firms included in the study are, in general, financial and deal with younger, more educated people.

Data security and *Data utilization* are issues of particular importance for service MNCs. The explanations for this finding centered on the differences between the business activities of service and manufacturing firms. *Data utilization* is an important concern for services because it is the business of services to process data and information, unlike manufacturing firms that produce a product. Services (especially financial ones) depend more directly on information about markets, information that is key to market trends, foreign exchange trading, and arbitrage opportunities. Information represents the means by which services make their money and, therefore, security and utilization of data become extremely important. Security also becomes more important when communication is electronic. To operate economically, it is usually not feasible to have dedicated or private lines, so protection of data becomes more essential when using shared lines.

GENERAL INTERNATIONAL VARIABLES

A number of company variables relating to the organization's international business operations may influence the significance of international IS issues. Level of international involvement has been shown to be an important variable and is defined in various ways (for example, foreign sales/total sales, foreign assets/total assets, and foreign employees/total employees). As discussed in Chapter 1, the firm goes through various stages of growth in its internationalization process. Depending on its position in this continuum, the firm's commitment to international business activities will likely influence the significance of international IS issues.

Other variables such as the number of foreign direct investments and the location of these subsidiaries may have significant implications for the transfer and management of IS technology. Problems encountered may be complicated by the multiplicity of countries involved. The interaction of many variables complicates business decision making for IS managers in the international environment. In the sections that follow, we will examine these variables in greater detail with emphasis on the differences that may exist for service and manufacturing MNCs.

Foreign Sales/Total Corporate Sales

The international IS issues study used foreign sales/total corporate sales as a measure of the firm's international involvement. Statistical analysis revealed a difference in responses for manufacturing firms at 25 percent foreign sales/total corporate sales.[14] Service firms were not evaluated on this variable since over 80 percent of the service firms in the sample had under 20 percent foreign sales. Table 3–3 depicts the rating of issues in terms of mean scores for manufacturing firms broken down at 25 percent foreign sales/total sales.

Three issues were identified that contribute most to this overall difference between manufacturing firms with 25 percent or over foreign sales/total sales and those with under 25 percent. These issues are *International MIS planning, Integrated services digital networks (ISDNs)* and *Integration of technologies*. These issues are highlighted in Table 3–4 and denoted by asterisks in Table 3–3.

It is expected that *International MIS planning* would contribute to a difference between these groups. However, explanations for the other issues are not as apparent. Again, opinions of interview participants

TABLE 3-3 Comparison of Means for Manufacturing Firms Split at 25% Foreign Sales/Total Sales

	Rank in Means of Issues for Manufacturing Firms Under 25% Foreign Sales/Total Sales		Rank in Means of Issues for Manufacturing Firms 25% or Over Foreign Sales/Total Sales	
Rank	Issue	Mean	Rank	Issue	Mean
1.	End-user computing	5.2667	* 1.	Integration of technologies	5.5714
2.	Educating senior personnel	5.2333	1.	Educating senior personnel	5.5714
3.	International protocol standards	5.1333	3.	International protocol standards	5.5429
4.	Use of information technology for competitive advantage	5.1000	* 4.	International MIS planning	5.2647
4.	Price and quality of telecommunications	5.1000	5.	Use of information technology for competitive advantage	5.2000
6.	Vendor support in foreign subsidiaries	4.9333	6.	Centralized/distributed processing	5.0286
* 7.	Integration of technologies	4.8621	6.	Price and quality of telecommunications technology	5.0286
* 8.	Integrated services digital networks (ISDNs)	4.8333	8.	Regulatory strategies of PTTs	4.9714
8.	Data security	4.8333	8.	Telecommunications deregulation	4.9714
8.	Local cultural constraints	4.8333	10.	End-user computing	4.9143
11.	Learning to conduct IS business in other countries	4.7667	10.	Data security	4.9143
12.	Aligning the IS organization	4.7333	12.	Data utilization	4.8857
13.	Regulatory strategies of PTTs	4.7000	13.	Aligning the IS organization	4.8286
14.	Centralization/distributed processing	4.6667	13.	Software development	4.8286
15.	Recruiting and training	4.6333	13.	Changes in telecommunications technology	4.8286
15.	Computer-integrated manufacturing	4.6333	16.	Recruiting and training	4.6286
17.	Telecommunications deregulation	4.5667	17.	Learning to conduct IS business in other countries	4.4857
17.	Changes in telecommunications technology	4.5667			

No.	Issue	Mean	No.	Issue	Mean
19.	Data utilization	4.5333	17.	Use of value added networks (VANs) by MNCs	4.4857
20.	Software development	4.4667	19.	Vendor support in foreign subsidiaries	4.4571
21.	Level of information technology sophistication in the country	4.2414	19.	Local cultural constraints	4.4571
22.	Legal restrictions on software/hardware acquisition	4.2333	21.	Computer integrated manufacturing	4.4286
23.	External data	4.1333	21.	Level of information technology sophistication in the country	4.4286
*24.	International MIS planning	4.1000	23.	Transborder data flow restrictions	4.3143
24.	Transborder data flow restrictions	4.1000	24.	Banned usage of telecommunications equipment	4.2000
26.	Banned usage of telecommunications equipment	3.9333	25.	Legal restrictions on hardware/software acquisition	4.1143
26.	Language barriers	3.9333	25.	External data	4.1143
28.	Use of value added networks (VANs) for MNCs	3.9310	*27.	Integrated services digital networks (ISDNs)	4.0857
29.	Interorganizational systems	3.8667	27.	Interorganizational systems	4.0857
30.	The national infrastructure	3.7667	29.	Language barriers	3.8571
31.	Export restrictions	3.7000	29.	The national infrastructure	3.8571
32.	Currency restrictions and exchange rate volatility	3.4000	31.	Export restrictions	3.6000
			32.	Currency restrictions and exchange rate volatility	3.3714

*These issues represent a statistically significant difference in response for manufacturing firms split at 25% foreign sales/total sales.

TABLE 3–4   Major Issues of Difference for Manufacturing Firms Split at 25% Foreign Sales/Total Sales

Issues
International MIS planning
Integrated services digital networks (ISDNs)
Integration of technologies

Source: P. Candace Deans, Kirk R. Karwan, Martin D. Goslar, David A. Ricks, and Brian Toyne, "Identification of Key International Information Systems Issues in U.S.-Based Multinational Corporations," *Journal of Management Information Systems* (vol. 7, no. 4, Spring 1991).

provide some helpful insights and are summarized in the paragraphs below. [15]

Table 3–3 shows that *International MIS planning* is rated issue number four for manufacturing MNCs with over 25 percent foreign sales/total sales, whereas it is rated number twenty-four for manufacturing firms with under 25 percent foreign sales. The international involvement of firms with under 25 percent foreign sales/total sales is generally not at a level for these firms to place particular emphasis on planning for their international information systems. For these firms, international IS planning is generally accomplished under the umbrella of domestic planning. Companies have, however, approached this issue in a variety of ways. In some cases, a business unit may be set up for international systems planning. In many service firms, a vice president for international information systems has been established. Another alternative may be to establish an international systems group that reports to one manager.

On the other hand, a majority of manufacturing firms with over 25 percent foreign sales/total sales have set up separate departments for international information systems. In other cases, there are managers responsible for different geographic areas worldwide, although there may be no separate division at the corporate level. Companies with limited international involvement that do not currently have some type of separate planning arrangement for international IS do foresee a move in this direction as they progress in their global business orientation.

Integrated services digital networks (ISDNs) is an issue currently receiving significant attention both domestically and internationally. Interestingly, manufacturing firms with limited international involvement perceive this issue to be of more importance than firms with greater international involvement (measured by foreign sales/total sales). Respondents provided consistent explanations for this result. It is felt that the larger companies can economically justify solving their own problems by implementing their own networks. They have more resources and staff and enough data traffic to support their own dedicated lines. For smaller companies looking for alternative networks, ISDNs may be an option. Since smaller companies cannot usually afford their own networks, they have to wait for ISDN standards.

Results depicted in Table 3–3 show that manufacturing firms with greater foreign sales consider *Integration of technologies* a higher priority issue than do firms with limited international involvement. The explanation given most often was that companies with greater foreign involvement are usually larger and further along in the stream of things (for instance, they operate in a multivendor environment, have acquired a lot of diverse technology, and operate in many different countries). Smaller companies with less foreign revenue are still looking at individual technology and trying to put in new systems. They are typically not as involved with as many countries and vendors and in many cases rely on only one vendor. Larger companies have their strategy in place and are looking to integrate their technology, whereas smaller companies may not have a cohesive plan. Smaller companies are more likely to be involved with joint ventures and not have as much control over day-to-day operations. Integrating technology will continue to be a concern because of the proliferation of products that are available.

Number of Foreign Subsidiaries

The number of foreign subsidiaries appears to have some relation to the nature of the firm's business, whether service or manufacturing. Based on the international IS issues study, and as shown in Table 3–5, a comparison of the number of foreign direct investments for service versus manufacturing firms reveals that manufacturing firms tend to own more foreign investments even though services may operate in many different countries. Since foreign direct investment requires direct participation in management of the foreign enterprise, this variable is likely to be a contributing factor in the difference in importance of issues for service and manufacturing firms.

TABLE 3-5 Number of Foreign Subsidiaries

Number of Foreign Subsidiaries	Service Industry (N = 46)	Manufacturing Industry (N = 65)
> 100	0.0%	13.9%
> 50 to 100	1.8%	13.8%
> 25 to 50	3.6%	21.5%
> 10 to 25	12.5%	23.1%
> 5 to 10	14.3%	16.9%
≤ 5	67.8%	10.8%

Source: P. Candace Deans, Kirk R. Karwan, Martin D. Goslar, David A. Ricks, and Brian Toyne, "Identification of Key International Information Systems Issues in U.S.-Based Multinational Corporations," *Journal of Management Information Systems* (vol. 7, no. 4, Spring 1991).

Location of Foreign Subsidiaries

Interviews with IS executives about the importance of various international IS issues strongly suggest that the location of the foreign investment may be more significant than the number of foreign investments. Firms with a wide distribution of foreign subsidiaries around the globe will likely have a greater array of concerns than firms with subsidiaries concentrated in one or two geographic regions. As mentioned previously, in some parts of the world it may take considerable time and effort to obtain basic services for telecommunications, if services are available at all. This may hinder efforts to globally integrate technology or provide means by which to set up a global network among all company locations on an international scale.

Multinationality

The firm's multinationality (that is, the number of countries in which the firm has subsidiaries) is directly linked to the number of foreign subsidiaries and the location of those subsidiaries. Companies that operate in many different countries will certainly encounter a multiplicity of government regulations, legal restrictions, economic and political conditions, and cultural climates. Variations in these conditions from one country to another may complicate the effective implementation of global information systems.

INTERNATIONAL ORGANIZATION VARIABLES

In this section we will examine more closely organizational character-istics (for example, international organization structure, international data processing operations, perceived strategic role of information sys-tems technology, and international experience). Our insights will facil-itate the evaluation of other possible factors contributing to the differences in importance of international IS issues for service and manufacturing firms.

International Data Processing Operations

Results of a study by Kane show that multinational companies organize their data processing operations differently domestically than they do internationally.[16] The Deans et al. research further supports the finding that companies view the tradeoffs of centralized, decentralized, and distributed processing alternatives differently for these two environ-ments.[17] In centralized systems, data processing takes place through a central company location, while decentralized systems provide for local processing with no central processor through which communications pass. Distributive systems allow for processing to take place in multiple machines through communication links between central and local points.

Based on results from Kane's study of U.S.-based multinational corporations, Table 3–6 shows a breakdown of domestic versus inter-national data processing operations. As exemplified in Table 3–6, do-mestic data processing operations tend toward centralized systems while a majority of international data processing is decentralized. Distributed systems have been implemented equally among domestic and interna-

TABLE 3–6 Data Processing Operations (%)

	United States	International
Centralized	42.5	16.8
Decentralized	30.8	59.1
Distributed	26.7	24.1
	100.0	100.0

Source: Michael J. Kane, *A Study of the Impact of Transborder Data Flow Regulation on Large United States-Based Corporations Using an Extended Information Systems Interface Model*, Ph.D. Dissertation, University of South Carolina, 1986, p. 86.

tional operations. Only a small percentage of respondents from this study use centralized systems internationally. Table 3–7 shows a further detailed representation of the comparison of international versus U.S. data processing alternatives. These results reveal that more firms have implemented decentralized systems for both their domestic and international operations. This is followed by those firms with centralized domestic operations and decentralized international processing. Other corporations either have all centralized or all distributed operations worldwide. Few firms fall in the other categories.

The international IS issues study evaluated international data processing operations based on a breakdown for service and manufacturing MNCs. Table 3–8 depicts these results and indicates that a majority of service firms tend toward centralized data processing operations while a majority of manufacturing firms tend toward decentralized operations internationally. It appears that international data processing operations may be contributing to the difference in the importance of the issues for service and manufacturing firms.

Table 3–9 shows an additional breakdown of international data processing operations for manufacturing firms split at 25 percent foreign sales/total sales. In terms of type of operations, manufacturing firms in this study tend toward an equal distribution for both centralized and decentralized alternatives. Although twice as many firms with over 25 percent foreign sales/total sales (10 to 5) have implemented distributed systems, these results seem to suggest that the type of data processing operations is not likely to contribute to the difference between these groups.

Manufacturing firms, regardless of the level of international involve-

TABLE 3 – 7   Data Processing Configurations (%)

United States	*International*		
	Centralized	*Decentralized*	*Distributed*
Centralized	12.21	22.14	6.87
Decentralized	0.76	27.48	3.82
Distributed	3.05	10.69	12.98

Source: Michael J. Kane, *A Study of the Impact of Transborder Data Flow Regulation on Large United States-Based Corporations Using an Extended Information Systems Interface Model,* Ph.D. Dissertation, University of South Carolina, 1986, p. 87.

TABLE 3-8 International Data Processing Operations by Firm Type

	Manufacturing	*Service*
Centralized	7	24
Decentralized	43	15
Distributed	15	7
Total	65	46

Source: P. Candace Deans, Kirk R. Karwan, Martin D. Goslar, David A. Ricks, and Brian Toyne, "Identification of Key International Information Systems Isues in U.S.-Based Multinational Corporations," *Journal of Management Information Systems* (vol. 7, no. 4, Spring 1991).

ment (measured by foreign sales/total sales), tend to agree that the only way to operate internationally is to decentralize. In contrast, from the perspective of the service MNC, centralized processing in the United States with delivery points in foreign countries makes it possible to avoid many of the issues that cause problems. For example, with centralized systems, foreign vendor problems can be avoided, and the primary concerns then become communications problems. The main advantages of centralized systems are the economy of scale and consistency of operations that result when centralized resources control the software.

Although very few firms have implemented distributed processing operations internationally, many IS executives agree that distributed systems offer the best of both centralized and decentralized systems.

TABLE 3-9 International Data Processing Operations by Foreign Sales/Total Sales for Manufacturing Firms

	Foreign Sales/Total Sales	
	Under 25%	*25% or Over*
Centralized	4	3
Decentralized	22	21
Distributed	5	10
Total	31	34

Source: P. Candace Deans, Kirk R. Karwan, Martin D. Goslar, David A. Ricks, and Brian Toyne, "Identification of Key International Information Systems Issues in U.S.-Based Multinational Corporations," *Journal of Management Information Systems* (vol. 7, no. 4, Spring 1991).

Most firms that have moved to distributed systems domestically, however, still perceive the problems to be too great and costly to implement these systems internationally. Firms with distributed international systems tend to have a core software package with a local systems support staff. Distributing includes greater production costs but the tradeoffs are gains in economy and network flexibility because local, and not common, requirements are duplicated. Although many argue that distributed systems are the ideal approach, for most firms it is currently not the most practical system internationally.[18]

International Organization Structure

International organization structure is patterned to a large degree after the domestic counterpart. The simplest type of international structure is one in which each group or division of the company independently accepts responsibility for its own international activity. Companies with greater international involvement may establish their own international division which must compete with other divisions for available resources. The international division may not, however, meet the needs of the firm as its international business expands. According to Korth, there are basically four global formats that a firm may consider: product orientation, functional orientation, geographical orientation, and customer orientation. A fifth format, matrix structure, is a hybrid of at least two of the other forms.[19]

Information flows and requirements will vary according to the firm's management structure. This structure is expected to play a significant role in the importance of international IS issues. Cash, McFarlan, and McKenney suggest that the organization structure may affect the level of information technology support that is required internationally.[20] Galbraith supports the view that information processing requirements are the primary determinants in selection of an organization structure.[21] Davidson points out that international divisions create a barrier to the transfer of technology of foreign subsidiaries.[22] Kane and Ricks consider the relationship between organization structure and the firm's assessment of transborder data flow regulation.[23]

An analysis by type of international organization structure (based on the Deans et. al. study) for manufacturing and service firms is provided in Table 3–10. A majority of service firms with limited international involvement have an international division structure. Manufacturing firms tend toward geographic area structure followed by international

TABLE 3-10 Type of International Organization Structure by Firm Type

	Manufacturing	*Service*
Geographic Area	24	6
Functional Area	5	8
Product Area	13	5
International Division	15	24
Matrix	4	5
Total	61	48

Source: P. Candace Deans, Kirk R. Karwan, Martin D. Goslar, David A. Ricks, and Brian Toyne, "Identification of Key International Information Systems Issues in U.S.-Based Multinational Corporations," *Journal of Management Information Systems* (vol. 7, no. 4, Spring 1991).

division and product area structures. The breakdown in Table 3-11 reveals that more manufacturing firms with under 25 percent foreign sales/total sales have an international division structure. As foreign involvement increases, the manufacturing firms in this study move toward geographic area and product area structures. These results tend to support the structural stages theory of Stopford and Wells, that with increased international involvement firms evolve from an international division structure to more complex structures.[24]

TABLE 3-11 Type of International Organization Structure by Foreign Sales/Total Sales for Manufacturing Firms

	Foreign Sales/Total Sales	
	Under 25%	*25% or Over*
Geographic Area	6	17
Functional Area	3	4
Product Area	6	7
International Division	11	4
Matrix	1	3
Total	27	35

Source: P. Candace Deans, Kirk R. Karwan, Martin D. Goslar, David A. Ricks, and Brian Toyne, "Identification of Key International Information Systems Issues in U.S.-Based Multinational Corporations," *Journal of Management Information Systems* (vol. 7, no. 4, Spring 1991).

Perceived Strategic Impact of Information Technology

As noted in Table 3–1, *Use of information technology for competitive advantage* in the international context is a top priority issue for both multinational service and manufacturing firms. According to Lucas and Turner, technology expands the range and number of strategic opportunities considered by the firm. By including technological considerations in the development of corporate strategy, the technology makes its maximum contribution to the organization.[25]

Table 3–12 outlines responses from service and manufacturing firms of the Deans et. al. study that concentrate on the perceived strategic role that information systems technology assumes in American corporations. Most service firms tend to view the role of IS technology as strategic to the firm (an application is strategic if it changes a firm's product or the way a firm competes in its industry). Manufacturing firms split on this response. The difference is likely a result of the type of business activity characteristic of service firms compared to that of manufacturing firms. For many service firms, information either is a product or is inseparable from the service the firm offers. For manufacturing firms, the product produced is usually a tangible good and information usually plays an ancillary role.

Categorized by foreign sales/total sales for manufacturing firms, it is interesting to note that a higher percentage of firms with under 25 percent foreign sales/total sales tend to perceive their information technology to be strategic to the organization. These results are presented in Table 3–13. Little can be concluded about the relationship between the perceived strategic impact of IS technology and the level of international involvement. Cash, McFarlan, and McKenney suggest that the

TABLE 3–12   Perceived Strategic Impact of Information Technology by Firm Type

	Manufacturing	*Service*
Nonstrategic	31	10
Strategic	33	44
Total	64	54

Source: P. Candace Deans, *The Transfer and Management of Information Systems (IS) Technology in the International Environment: Identification of Key Issues for MIS Managers in U.S.-Based Multinational Corporations*, Ph.D. Dissertation, University of South Carolina, 1989.

TABLE 3-13 Perceived Strategic Impact of Information Technology by Foreign Sales/Total Sales for Manufacturing Firms

| | Foreign Sales/Total Sales | | | |
| | Under 25% | | 25% or Over | |
	%	Actual	%	Actual
Nonstrategic	36.7%	11	55.9%	19
Strategic	63.3%	19	44.1%	15
Total	100%	30	100%	34

Source: P. Candace Deans, *The Transfer and Management of Information Systems (IS) Technology in the International Environment: Identification of Key Issues for MIS Managers in U.S.-Based Multinational Corporations*, Ph.D. Dissertation, University of South Carolina, 1989.

nature of the firm's business may play the most significant role in determining the strategic impact of information technology.[26] The data in the table indicate that perceived strategic impact of IS technology does not appear to be related to increased foreign involvement.

International Experience

International experience is another variable that deserves some mention both in terms of the firm's international business experience in general and in terms of the company's experience with the implementation of information systems internationally. It may be argued that international involvement is a surrogate for international business experience. On the other hand, there may be a case for separation of these variables. According to Terpstra and Yu, the firm's international experience may prompt changes in the firm's organization structure as well as in its information-gathering and assessing systems.[27]

Cash, McFarlan, and McKenney emphasize the importance of the firm's experience with the technology.[28] They argue that management concerns, control, and technology transfer acquire greater significance as the firm's experience with the technology increases. In the early phases of technological learning, the firm may be preoccupied with using the technology and experimenting with applications of potential benefit to the organization.

It is our conclusion that the firm's international business experience and specific experience with information technology have an impact on the importance of international information systems issues to the firm.

SUMMARY

As we move toward a more service-oriented economy domestically, it has become necessary to look more closely at the concerns of the service sector. These concerns may be quite different from those of the traditional manufacturing firm. Internationally, services are continuing to grow and are becoming a significant component of world business.

As emphasized in this chapter, multinational manufacturing and service firms differ on a number of international characteristics. In general, manufacturing firms tend to be more involved internationally in foreign subsidiaries, level of foreign sales, and the number of countries and locations in which they do business. Manufacturing and service MNCs also differ in terms of a number of other factors related to international organization characteristics such as international data processing, international organization structure, and the perceived strategic impact of information technology to the firm.

Differences in the importance of IS issues between multinational manufacturing firms and service firms appear to be due in large part to the nature of the business. In service firms, their business is largely information processing. In manufacturing firms, processing of information plays an important support role but is usually not the focus of the firm's business. Another contributing factor to the difference in the importance of the issues for these two groups is the fact that service firms are generally not as involved internationally (that is, they do not have as many foreign subsidiaries or operate in as many different countries). Services also tend to centralize their data-processing operations on an international basis, whereas manufacturing firms tend to decentralize them.

Differences in the importance of the issues for manufacturing firms split at 25 percent foreign sales/total sales appear to be due in part to the size of the corporation. Companies with greater foreign involvement are generally larger companies and are more likely to have financial resources that make more alternatives available. These companies have usually been involved internationally for a longer period of time and operate in more countries. These companies have learned to deal with many of the international obstacles that smaller companies are still in the process of addressing.

NOTES

1. D. Bell, "Notes on the Post-Industrial Society," in *Search for Alternatives: Public Policy and the Study of the Future*, ed. F. Tugwell (Massachusetts: Winthrop Publishers, 1973).

2. Peter F. Drucker, "The Coming of the New Organization," *Harvard Business Review* (January–February 1988): 45–53.

3. Ibid., 45.

4. Lyman W. Porter and Lawrence E. McKibbin, *Management Education and Development: Drift or Thrust into the 21st Century?* (New York: McGraw-Hill, Inc., 1988), 23–24.

5. Michael R. Czinkota and Ilkka A. Ronkainen, *International Marketing*, 2nd ed. (Chicago: The Dryden Press, 1990), Chapter 12, 677.

6. Ibid., 680–681.

7. Ibid.

8. Valerie A. Zeithami, A. Parasuraman, and Leonard L. Berry, "Problems and Strategies in Services Marketing," *Journal of Marketing* (Spring 1985): 33–46.

9. John E. Bateson, "Why We Need Service Marketing," in *Conceptual and Theoretical Developments in Marketing* (Chicago: American Marketing, 1979), 131–146.

10. Vern Terpstra and Chwo-Ming Yu, "Determinants of Foreign Investment of U.S. Advertising Agencies," *Journal of International Business Studies* (Spring 1988): 33–46.

11. P. Candace Deans, Kirk R. Karwan, Martin D. Goslar, David A. Ricks, and Brian Toyne, "Identification of Key International Information Systems Issues in U.S.-Based Multinational Corporations," *Journal of Management Information Systems* (vol. 7, no. 4, Spring 1991), 46.

12. Ibid., 35.

13. Ibid., 40.

14. Ibid., 35.

15. Ibid., 42–43.

16. Michael J. Kane, "*A Study of the Impact of Transborder Data Flow Regulations on Large United States-Based Corporations Using an Extended Information Systems Interface Model*," (Ph.D. dissertation, University of South Carolina, 1986), 85–90.

17. Deans et. al., 42.

18. Ibid., 35.

19. Christopher M. Korth, *International Business Environment and Management* (New Jersey: Prentice Hall, Inc., 1985), 365–380.

20. James I. Cash, Warren F. McFarlan, and James L. McKenney, *Corporate Information Systems Management* (Illinois: Irwin Publishing Company, 1988), 220.

21. J. R. Galbraith, "Organizational Design: An Information Processing View," *Interfaces* (Fall 1974): 28–36.

22. William H. Davidson, *Global Strategic Management* (New York: John Wiley and Sons, 1982).

23. Michael J. Kane and David A. Ricks, "Is Transnational Data Flow Regulation a Problem?" *Journal of International Business Studies* (Fall 1988): 477–482.

24. John Stopford and Lewis Wells, *Managing the Multinational Enterprise* (New York: Basic Books, 1972).

25. Henry C. Lucas and Jon A. Turner, "A Corporate Strategy for the Control of Information Processing," *Sloan Management Review* (Fall 1982): 25–36.

26. Cash, McFarlan, and McKenney, 220.

27. Terpstra and Yu, 33–46.

28. Cash, McFarlan, and McKenney, 26–27.

STUDY QUESTIONS

1. Assume the role of vice president of international information systems for a major U.S.-based bank. Discuss how IS issues and concerns for your operations may be different from those confronting a large multinational manufacturing firm.

2. Discuss the significance of international MIS planning and integration of technology from the perspective of the large manufacturing firm with substantial international involvement (over 50 percent foreign sales/total sales) as compared to a smaller manufacturer with limited international involvement (less than 25 percent foreign sales/total sales).

3. Discuss other general international variables from the perspective of the organization that may influence the importance of international IS issues.

4. How do multinational service and manufacturing firms generally differ in terms of international data processing operations, international organization structure, and perceptions of the strategic importance of information technology to the firm?

5. Based on data collected to date, what can be concluded about the relationship between the level of foreign sales/total sales and the manufacturing

MNCs international data processing operations and international organization structure?

6. How might the firm's international business experience in general and specific experience with information systems technology internationally influence the importance of IS issues?

SUGGESTED READINGS

Albrecht, Karl. *At America's Service*. Illinois: Dow Jones-Irwin, 1988.

Albrecht, Karl, and Lawrence J. Bradford. *The Service Advantage*. Illinois: Dow Jones-Irwin, 1989.

Boddewyn, Jean J., Marsha Halbrich, and A. C. Perry. "Service Multinationals: Conceptualization, Measurement and Theory." *Journal of International Business Studies* (Fall 1986): 41–57.

Deans, P. Candace. "The Transfer and Management of Information Systems (IS) Technology in the International Environment: Identification of Key Issues for MIS Managers in U.S.-Based Multinational Corporations." Ph.D. dissertation, University of South Carolina, 1989.

Drucker, Peter. *The New Realities*. New York: Harper & Row, 1989.

Giarini, Orio, ed. *The Emerging Service Economy*. Oxford: Paragon Press, 1987.

Hackett, Gregory P. "Investment in Technology—The Service Sector Sinkhole?" *Sloan Management Review* (Winter 1990): 97–103.

Mowery, David C., ed. *International Collaborative Ventures in U.S. Manufacturing*. Massachusetts: Ballinger, 1988.

Naisbitt, John, and Patricia Aburdene. *Ten New Directions for the 1990s*. New York: William Morrow & Co., 1990.

Noori, Hamid. *Managing the Dynamics of New Technology: Issues in Manufacturing Management*. New Jersey: Prentice Hall, 1990.

Quinn, James Brian, and Penny C. Pacquette. "Technology in Services: Creating Organizational Revolutions." *Sloan Management Review* (Winter 1990): 67–78.

Quinn, James Brian, Thomas L. Doorley, and Penny C. Pacquette. "Technology in Services: Rethinking Strategic Focus." *Sloan Management Review* (Winter 1990): 79–87.

Shaw, John C. *The Service Focus: Developing Winning Game Plans for Service Companies*. Illinois: Dow Jones-Irwin, 1990.

Chapter F O U R

Transnational Flows of Data and Information

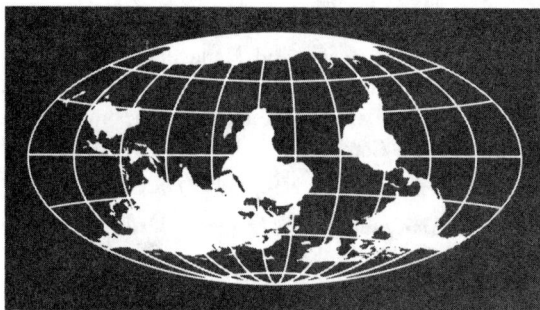

International transfers of information have existed since man first began to venture outside his native borders. Perhaps the most famous transfer of information occurred when Miltiades defeated the Persians at the battle of Marathon in 490 B.C. After the battle, a runner was dispatched to carry the news of victory back to the awaiting Athenians so that preparations could be made for the return of Miltiades' triumphant army.[1] Our modern-day Olympic marathon originated from this twenty-six-mile transfer of information. Today, transborder data flow (TDF) is viewed as a potential threat to the sovereignty of the modern nation-state. At the same time, TDF is the operational lifeblood of the multinational corporation. Why has this age-old phenomenon received so much attention and debate?

The answer may be found in the ongoing shift from a world economy based almost totally on production to one in which over half of the world's gross domestic product is generated by information-related jobs. In this chapter we will discuss the nature and evolution of transborder data flows, the concerns and regulations of host country governments, the impact of TDF regulation on the operations of multinational companies, and the management strategies employed in large MNCs to comply with these regulations while maintaining control and coordination of the firm's international operations.

THE NATURE OF TRANSBORDER DATA FLOWS

Transborder data flows are widely discussed in both government and business circles, but often the terms and definitions used in the debate are rather poorly defined, leading to misinterpretation and misunderstanding.

The definition of *transborder data flow* (TDF) can be interpreted in a narrow or broad context. In a narrow context, it refers to data that are stored and transmitted via computer and telecommunication networks. In broad usage, TDF refers to all data and information that cross a national border in any way or form. It can refer to raw data stored in machine-readable format or to television programs produced and transmitted from one country to another. With the growing use of facsimile machines, personal computers, and CD-ROM technology, the broader definition of TDF is gaining acceptance. However, the narrow definition of TDF as the "movements of machine-readable data for processing, storage, or retrieval across national boundaries" is used most often.[2]

It is estimated that over 1,500 computer-communication networks are generating TDFs around the word.[3] These global information networks provide the infrastructure for the transmission of information from one country to another. Two fundamental functions provided by these networks are remote computing and data transfer.

Remote computing enables end users to access data processing facilities in other countries via telecommunications equipment and software. One provider of remote-computing services is General Electric Corporation, which operates the GE Information Service (GEIS). GEIS provides customers around the world with a variety of network-based services for message switching, electronic mail, systems integration, and electronic data interchange. For example, GEIS markets an electronic data interchange service called EDI*EXPRESS.™ General Motors and their subsidiary, EDS, are using this service to electronically exchange invoices, product specifications, and delivery schedules among over

2,000 automotive parts suppliers in six European countries. In France and Great Britain, General Motors is using France Telecom and Istel to provide the network services needed to link to their suppliers in those countries. Collectively, these network services made available by another company are known as *value added networks* or VANs.

The second function associated with TDF is data transfer. Data transfer enables end users in one country to access and retrieve information from databases located in other countries. Weather, news, and medical, financial, economic, and scientific information are regularly transferred and disseminated using VANs. Many companies such as IBM, Ford, and American Express operate private, internal networks. For example, IBM operates an internal network that allows researchers in its Hursley, England lab twenty-four-hour access to technical data stored in databases located in its San Jose, California manufacturing facility. The same system facilitates the exchange of personnel, financial, news, and other internal company data. Transborder data flows using either remote computing or data transfer are facilitated by third-party vendors such as GEIS, or private, internal networks.

The Evolution of TDF

The evolution and growth of transborder data flows are the result of two parallel developments: the merging of telecommunications and data processing technology and the evolution of the multinational corporation (MNC).

The 1950s marked the first successful entry of computers into the commercial environment. The initial application of this technology was specific to various accounting functions in the corporation. These applications facilitated the efficient flow of financial information throughout the organization, contributing timely and accurate information to the management decision-making process. The rapid development of new hardware and software technology soon enabled corporations to apply information systems to other areas, including order-entry, shipping and receiving, inventory control, and material production. Information technology not only helped decrease operating costs but also provided management with relevant information to make more-informed decisions.

In the late 1960s and early 1970s, telecommunications technology made great strides in increased capability and reduced cost. Telecommunications provided the manager with instantaneous access to data located in other computing facilities anywhere in the world. As a result, decision making no longer needs to be concentrated at the point of data collection and processing. Information technology has permitted the two tasks to reside even farther apart. The merging of telecommunications and data processing technologies has created transborder data flows in the modern sense of the term.

During this same period of computer-communications technology development, U.S. manufacturers continued to increase their level of foreign direct investment by establishing branch offices, distribution centers, research labs, and production facilities abroad. Service firms such as banks, advertising agencies, insurance companies, and accounting firms also expanded abroad to support their U.S. clients. The resulting expansion in the scope of the firm's operations and level of capital invested abroad made it important for headquarters management to have timely and accurate information concerning their international operations. This was particularly important because most MNCs implemented globally integrated strategies through a centralized decision-making process. The flow of data across national borders allowed management to better coordinate and control its worldwide activities and as a result, maximize its scarce resources. Information technology has given the MNC a tool capable of providing a competitive advantage over the purely domestic companies in the host country market.

Establishing overseas computing capability during the 1960s and 1970s was not an easy task for U.S.-based multinational corporations. Many host countries lacked the required communication and data processing infrastructure, personnel, and expertise to provide the needed systems to facilitate TDFs. These MNCs looked to other U.S. providers of computer and communications systems and services. But, unlike the United States, most countries provide communication services through a government-owned or controlled organization called the *postal, telephone, and telegraph* (PTT) agency.

The PTTs are responsible for three telecommunications areas: First, setting the tariff or pricing for a variety of communication services; second, developing and maintaining new telecommunications systems; third, controlling the use of these systems for transborder data flows.

Unfortunately, the development of modern telecommunications facilities in most countries, particularly less-developed countries, has lagged considerably behind that of the United States. This has made it very difficult for American MNCs to develop sophisticated, worldwide information networks.

The PTTs, in an effort to increase revenue in the early 1970s, leased their communication lines to private companies that provide *value-added networks* (VANs). These companies coupled the leased lines with their own sophisticated switching and packet facilities to enhance the capabilities of the network. In turn, they resold these services to other companies operating computer, telex, and internal communication networks. VANs provided the latest technology at a reasonable cost to their users. Instead of leasing single lines from the PTTs, the VAN systems allowed multiple users on the same leased line, thus reducing the cost to the individual user. Over time, the PTTs were unable to derive sufficient revenues to continue the development of new systems. In an effort to gain control over usage and increase their revenue base, the PTTs began implementing volume-sensitive tariffs and forcing the usage of public networks in order to monitor data traffic.

The effects of PTT policies and actions on the multinational corporation include the following: (1) an almost ten-fold increase in communications cost to the corporate user in some countries, (2) time delays in system licensing and approval, and (3) unavailability of the leading-edge technology. As a result, implementing global information systems has become a difficult and costly process for multinational organizations.

MNC OPERATIONS AND TRANSBORDER DATA FLOWS

The movement of data across national borders is as fundamental to operations of a multinational corporation as electricity is to our modern society. Without timely and accurate information, the executives of large global enterprises simply cannot function. The importance of information flows, particularly in the service industries such as banking and transportation, is expressed by one U.S. bank manager who states that "if we can't move data, we go out of business."[4] Worldwide information flows are a major concern for managers who must comply with a plethora of new regulations and restrictions on transborder data flows. To better understand the effects of these rules, we need to first understand the nature and patterns of information flows within the multinational organization.

Typical Information Flows

Multinational corporation headquarters depend on two types of information flows to manage their operations: flows of internal operating data and flows of external trade and economic data. Figure 4–1 depicts the

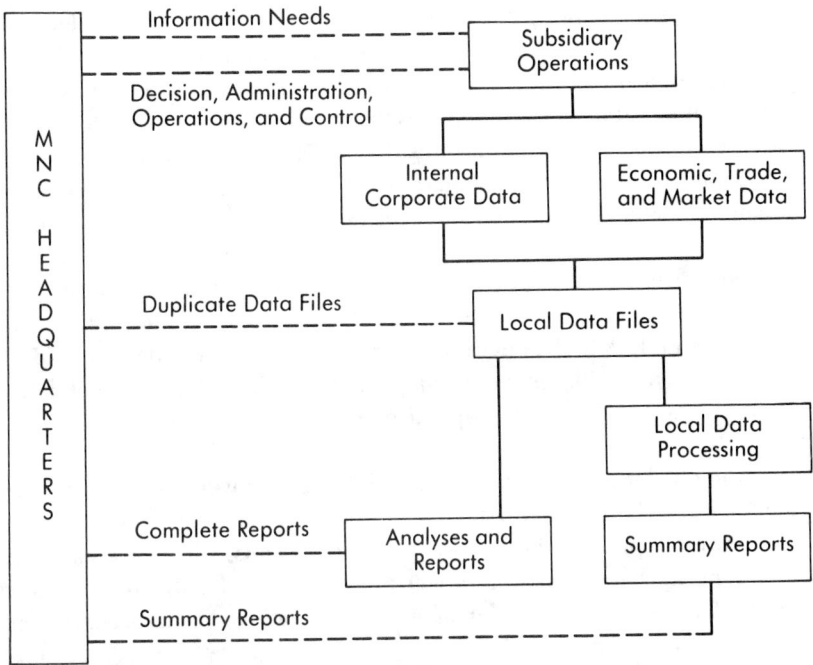

FIGURE 4-1   Typical Information Flow between an MNC Headquarters and Its Subsidiary

Source: Saeed, Samiee, "Transnational Data Flow Constraints: A New Challenge for Multinational Corporations," *Journal of International Business Studies* (Spring 1984): 142.

flow of information between a multinational corporate headquarters and its operating subsidiaries. The volume, type of information, and frequency of transmission are often determined by the type of industry, size of the firm, organization structure, and location of the corporate subsidiary.

As the figure shows, there are five channels of information and data exchange between an MNC headquarters and its subsidiary. The MNC subsidiary receives many information requests from headquarters. At the same time, corporate management sends the subsidiary operation a steady stream of decisions, guidelines, and policies related to administration and control. In return, the subsidiary sends transborder data flows in the form of raw data from duplicate databases, and a wide range of detailed and summary reports back to the parent organization. National government regulations that interfere with any of these transborder data flows can have a substantial impact on the operations of the MNC.

Research in the area of international information systems has identified four key linkages or interfaces that facilitate the flow of information between a parent firm and its subsidiary.[5] These components, as shown in Figure 4–2, include an organization, technical, data, and communication linkage. The organization component defines the planning, control, and support of the information systems linkage. The technical component is concerned with the issue of hardware and software compatibility between headquarter and subsidiary data centers. The data component refers to data definitions, record layouts, and database specifications. The communication component describes the level and detail of the transactions and the type of processing—either real-time or on-line.

The regulations and procedures used by host governments to monitor and control the transborder data flow activities of the multinational corporation represent three types of barriers or obstacles: cost, privacy, and control. These barriers reflect the economic, legal, political, and cultural issues of transborder data flow regulation discussed earlier in the chapter.

Obstacles and Barriers Encountered

Domestic and multinational corporations rely on their MIS departments to design, develop, and maintain information systems that facilitate the collection, storage, and flow of information in the enterprise. Figure 4–2 presents the extended information systems interface model. The model represents the major information system linkages between the parent firm and its subsidiary and the barriers or obstacles to these linkages that are created by transborder data flow regulation.

Research using the extended information systems linkage model in large U.S.-based multinational corporations has identified a number of problems encountered with TDF regulation. The problems presented in Table 4–1 are categorized by the type of barrier and the linkage element that it affects most. As the table indicates, most of the TDF regulation problems encountered by multinational corporations create a cost or control barrier between the parent and the subsidiary. These obstacles or barriers primarily affect the communication and data linkage elements of the international information system.

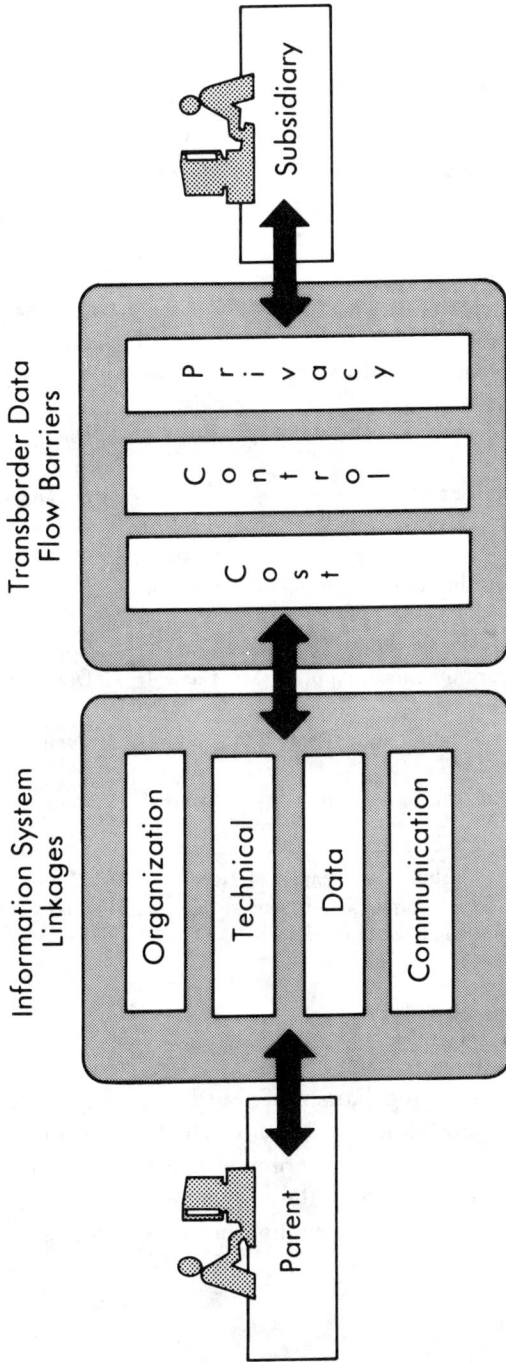

FIGURE 4–2 The Extended Information System Interface Model

Source: Michael J. Kane, "A Study of the Impact of Transborder Data Flow Regulation on Large United States-Based Corporations Using an Extended Information Systems Interface Model," unpublished dissertation, University of South Carolina, 1986, p. 54.

TABLE 4-1   TDF Problems Encountered by MNCs

TDF Problem Encountered	TDF Barrier	IS Linkage Element
Required use of locally manufactured data processing equipment, communication services, and software	Cost	Communication, technical
Processing of certain types of data locally	Privacy, control	Organization, data
Restrictions on the options for transmitting data from a host country	Control	Communication
Prohibited on-line connection to certain data bases	Privacy	Data, communication
Lengthy delays in acquiring leased lines	Control	Organization, communication
Increased tariffs	Cost	Communication
Contaminated data resulting from government monitoring procedures	Control	Data
Threat of a tax on the value of data	Cost	Communication
Prohibited out-of-country maintenance of application software programs	Control	Organization
Restricted use of full communications systems functions	Control	Communication
Required registration of data bases and systems	Control, privacy	Data

Source: Michael J. Kane, "A Study of the Impact of Transborder Data Flow Regulation on Large United States-Based Corporations Using an Extended Information Systems Interface Model," unpublished dissertation, University of South Carolina, 1986, p. 120.

Management Strategies for TDF

The managers of multinational enterprises use one or more strategies to comply with host country regulations of transborder data flows. One strategy is to monitor procedures to keep abreast of new regulations and to anticipate future, host country government legislation. Another is to take specific action to comply with the regulations and to address the impact of transborder data flow regulation on the corporation's operations.

TDF Monitoring Practices

To monitor activities of the firm, a wide range of approaches is used by management. Some multinational corporations have established an internal task force to assess the impact of transborder data flow regulation in each country where the firm conducts business. In other firms, the telecommunications manager studies the impacts of these regulations. In the latter case, the manager remains informed through professional journals, specialized reports, and other periodical literature. Most of these managers also belong to professional associations such as the Data Processing Management Association and the International Telecommunications User Group in which they share information about regulations. Interestingly, some large, money-center banks employ someone full time to monitor and insure compliance with regulations. As part of an overall political risk-assessment program, this person often reports to the government affairs department instead of the MIS department. However, this person usually possesses a strong knowledge of telecommunication concepts and a good working relationship with the MIS department.

Figures 4–3 and 4–4 present survey responses of 152 MIS executives in large U.S.-based multinationals concerning the impact of TDF regulation on their organizations. The data indicate that over half (53.0%) of the respondents have formally studied the impact of TDF regulation on their operations, and approximately one-fifth (20.4%) have implemented policy/procedure changes to address the impact of TDF regulation.

Successful TDF Strategies

The management strategies designed to monitor and address the impact of TDF regulation vary widely. The strategies are usually dependent on the firm's level of international business activity and the scope of the firm's international information systems operation. As depicted in Figure 4–5, the management strategies used to address the impact of TDF regulation center on five management practices.

Strategy 1: Reorganization of Data Processing

Historically, multinational corporations have controlled their international operations through a highly centralized management structure in which they organize their international operations as a separate international division. This is also true of the data processing area that supports the international division. Many corporate MIS groups have centralized control through large databases maintained at the headquarters. Central control also includes centralized application devel-

"Have You Studied the Impact of TDF Regulation on the Firm's Operations?"

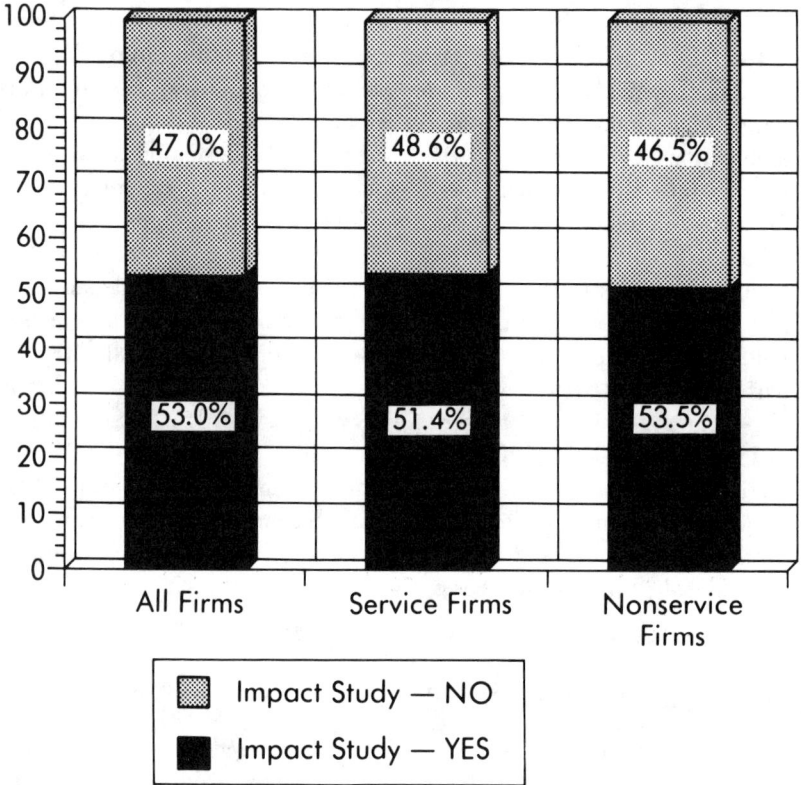

FIGURE 4-3   Management Response to TDF Regulation: Survey of MIS Executives in U.S. MNCs
Source: Michael J. Kane and David A. Ricks, "The Impact of Transborder Data Flow Regulation on Large United States-Based Corporations," *Columbia Journal of World Business* (Summer 1989): 24.

opment teams and technical support staffs to support a large mainframe operation.

In an attempt to address not only transborder data flow regulation but changing technology and end-user needs as well, the data processing operations of most multinational corporations are becoming more decentralized on a geographic basis. This is accomplished using distributed

"Have You Implemented Policy/Procedure Changes to Address the Impact of TDF Regulations?"

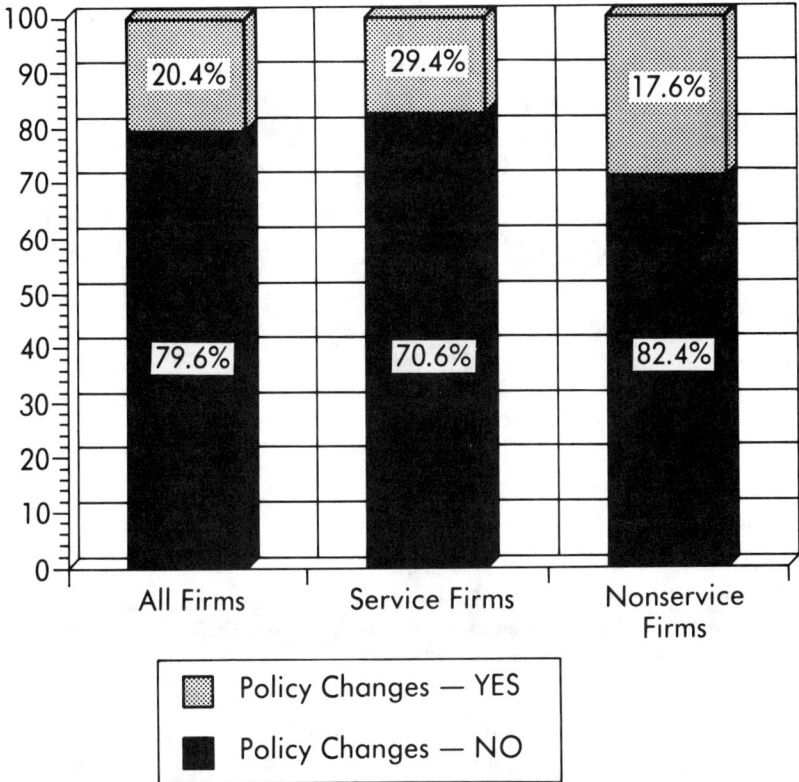

FIGURE 4-4 Management Response to TDF Regulation: Survey of MIS Executives in U.S. MNCs
Source: Michael J. Kane and David A. Ricks, "The Impact of Transborder Data Flow Regulation on Large United States-Based Corporations," *Columbia Journal of World Business* (Summer 1989): 24.

processing concepts to provide local computing capability while maintaining the flow of information to a central headquarters facility. This technique reflects a broad management philosophy aimed at addressing a number of opportunities and concerns in addition to transborder data flow regulation. Distributed systems enable the firm to standardize application software while giving each subsidiary greater control over its

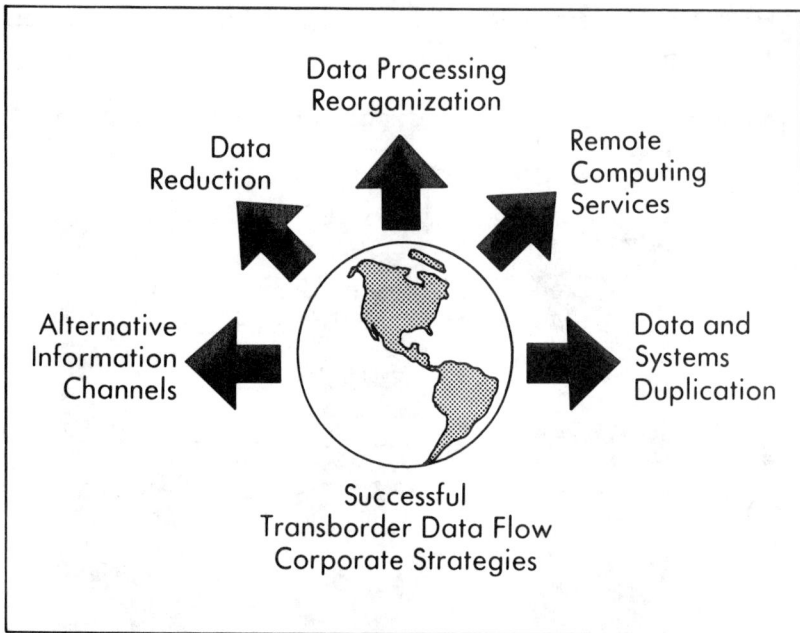

FIGURE 4-5 TDF Management Strategies and Practices

Source: Adapted from Michael J. Kane and David A. Ricks, "The Impact of Transborder Data Flow Regulation on Large United States-Based Corporations," *Columbia Journal of World Business* (Summer 1989): 27.

local computing needs. For example, to address the impact of local processing requirements and data privacy regulations, one of three system architectures can be implemented. First, a highly integrated distributed processing operation can be established that includes compatible hardware/software components operated by local users. Application development, technical support, and problem resolution responsibilities are located at either the headquarters data center or regional data centers. Second, a stand-alone systems approach can be set up in which each country has its own complete data processing operation with control over application development and technical support. In countries such as Brazil, restrictions on the use of non-Brazilian computer equipment make equipment compatibility a problem. This option is also desirable because the national government requires a substantial amount of local processing. A third option is a hybrid distributed system, which provides a middle ground between the other two approaches. The actual structure of the system will reflect the degree of autonomy given to local management and the degree of regulatory restrictions as well as a plethora of other factors, including the level of foreign investment, the amount of required data flows, the availability of equipment and staffing, and cost considerations.

Strategy 2: Remote Computing Services

In some multinational corporations, techniques address specific information system linkage elements affected by transborder data flow regulation. One example is the use of public communications facilities instead of private, internally operated leased lines. As previously discussed, transborder data flows take two forms, either as processed information or raw data. The flows of raw data across national borders are often more highly scrutinized by the local PTT authority and are the object of TDF regulation.

Many MNCs use the services of remote computing vendors such as General Electric's GEIS subsidiary to preprocess the raw data before sending it out of the country. While this reduces some control over data security, the corporation is less susceptible to the problems associated with transborder data flow regulation. Processing the data via a remote computing vendor, then transmitting the information abroad in summary form, often solves the processing and storage problems of certain types of data such as personnel records, credit information, and competitor information.

Strategy 3: Data Reduction

The third strategy for reducing the impact of TDF regulation is the systematic analysis of information flows and the elimination of unnecessary data. This strategy acknowledges that much of the data stored in automated systems does not enhance management decision making and should not be retained. Often this information consists of name-linked data that are subject to transborder data flow regulations. By eliminating the need to transmit these data, the corporation can comply with the host country's regulations and save the resources used to collect, store, and maintain those records.

Data reduction is carried out in a variety of ways. Most commonly, it is part of an on-going standards and documentation effort, which is responsible for the documentation of the firm's application programs, system procedures, data requirements, and report distribution lists. In conjunction with this function, users of information system reports that contain information subject to transborder data flow regulations are regularly asked to decide on the necessity of receiving that information. If the report is not needed, it is eliminated. If the report can be consolidated or redefined to meet compliance requirements, the MIS group performs this task.

An alternative method in the data reduction strategy employs a designated TDF specialist. If a corporation has assigned someone to this responsibility, part of the assignment usually entails documenting existing transborder data flows in the organization. This person may also be responsible for eliminating unnecessary and/or redundant transborder data flow as part of a corporate compliance program.

Data reduction is tedious work and can be quite costly in terms of manpower and application redesign work. It requires a great deal of high-level management involvement, given the dynamic nature of a firm's reporting requirements. Very few companies use data reduction as the primary vehicle to address the impact of transborder data flow. The best use of this strategy is in planning for future information systems and applications.

Strategy 4: Alternative Information Channels

Following a similar approach to data reduction strategy, some MNCs make use of alternative information channels to reduce the firm's transborder data flow requirements. This approach includes both automated and nonautomated procedures.

When TDFs are manipulated by a corporate staff before appearing in report form, there is an opportunity for the reduction of transborder data flows. For example, in one corporate personnel system, individual employee records are transmitted as raw data and the data is then consolidated in such a way that individual records are not distinguishable. In this case, shifting the staff activity to the subsidiary prior to transmission of the information to headquarters enables the firm to comply with the data privacy laws of the host country.

Alternatives to the intermediate processing of the data before they leave the country include the use of telex facilities and courier services. In the case of couriers, the data could reside on magnetic media or in the form of printed documents, depending on the individual country's regulations. These practices are difficult for the PTTs to control and must be enforced through customs officials rather than PTT representatives.

Strategy 5: Data and Systems Duplication

Another strategy used by large multinational corporations involves the duplication of databases. This approach is feasible because of the continuing trend of decreased per unit cost of data storage systems. Given the dramatic reduction in the cost per gigabyte (one billion bytes) of storage, duplication of large databases is economically justified. By duplicating certain types of data, the corporation can comply with local data protection laws and still facilitate the flow of information across national borders. As long as the original data reside in the host country, the firm may be considered in compliance of certain TDF regulations.

In most cases, the duplication of a database includes the accompanying application programs used to update and access the data. These systems are standardized so that control over the quality of the reporting is maintained. One corporation mixed this strategy with the data processing reorganization strategy to achieve its desired results. Since the firm wanted to maintain complete compatibility among its hardware/software components, it duplicated several information systems, making them resident in each subsidiary. It did so because host country regulations required the use of locally produced equipment when utilizing smaller computer systems. By enlarging the data processing center and its computer power, the corporation was able to replace the small computer system with a high-powered mainframe that was compatible with the headquarters information system. As a result of increasing the local computing power of the subsidiary, the firm was able to avoid restrictive government regulations.

KEY ISSUES CONCERNING TDF

The information technology providing worldwide information networks and their information flows has brought many concerned organizations into the international debate over the role and purpose of these networks and their information flows. Organizations include host and home country governments and regulatory agencies, multinational corporations, and various international, quasi-governmental organizations—each with legitimate concerns and differing perspectives. The seriousness of these issues is reflected in a Canadian report that urges its government to "act immediately to regulate transborder data flows to ensure that we do not lose control of information vital to the maintenance of national sovereignty."[6]

The major problems associated with transborder data flows result from two conditions: first, a rapid growth in the volume and type of TDF; second, the unbalanced nature of trade in information goods and services among nations of the world—in particular, the trade balance between developed and developing nations. The less-developed nations of the world view themselves as predominantly exporters of data and importers of finished information goods and services. Some developed nations view the United States in the same way.

While many host governments seek to control the economic-related activity of MNCs through the regulation of transborder data flows, the issues originate from an earlier concern: data privacy protection. The flow of personal, name-linked information from one country to another causes great concern among many nation-states for three primary reasons. First, it is felt that corporate decisions concerning individuals of one country should not be made in other countries. This is particularly true in relation to credit and individual financial data which contain a substantial amount of information concerning the private affairs of a country's citizens. Second, many believe that computers are subject to great misuse given the difficulty in adequately safeguarding access to large databases. Third, the data collected via automated systems may lack relevance and quality as the basis for making decisions concerning individuals. While data privacy is still a concern today, it is not the only issue which comprises the transborder data flow debate. Cultural, legal, political, and economic aspects are of equal concern to those directly involved in regulation and compliance.

The MNC is often the target of TDF regulation because it is not only a provider of the computer-telecommunication infrastructure but also a prime facilitator of its accompanying data flows. This places the corporation directly in the middle of the debate. As shown in Figure 4–6, host country government concerns related to transborder data flows can be categorized as economic, legal, political, and cultural.

The issues presented in Figure 4–6 are the direct or indirect result of information collected or generated in one country and sent across national borders to another country. The economic issues related to transborder data flows include the development and protection of a nation's data processing industry. Sending data out of the country for

Economic	• Protection of infant industries • Loss of revenue to data-processing industry • Volume-sensitive pricing of TDFs • Taxation based on data value

Legal	• Individual privacy protection • European common law vs. U.S. civil law • Omnibus legislation vs. sectoral legislation

Political	• National policy for informatics • Loss of national sovereignty • U.S. dominance of information technology markets

Cultural	• Preservation of a national identity

FIGURE 4-6 Concerns of Host Country Governments Related to Transborder Data Flows

processing and storage limits the domestic market for information products and services and thus limits the development of that nation's domestic capabilities. There is also a growing realization that data has economic value as an export commodity. Governments therefore feel that they should tax or restrict transborder data flows through the use of tariffs.

The legal issues associated with TDFs focus on the privacy protection of individual citizens. The problems in this area tend to be the result of different legal systems and approaches to regulation enforced by national governments. These differences lead to the restriction of transborder data flows for reasons of legal reciprocity and compatibility.

There are three areas of political concern to host governments regarding transborder data flows. These include the development of a national policy for informatics, a loss of national sovereignty, and the perception that the United States dominates information technology markets. In many ways, these issues can be viewed in a broader context of developed nations versus less-developed nations. Many host governments view information as a national resource like gold, oil, or wood. The less-developed nations export raw data in the same way they export natural resources. In return, they import finished products in the form of information products and services. Host country governments believe the result of this dependence on developed countries for information technology is a loss of national sovereignty and economic security, which demand that a national information policy be developed to protect this vital resource.

From a cultural perspective, many countries see the influence of imported television and radio programming as a detriment to their society's preservation of a national identity. When broadly defined, transborder data flow is the primary means for cultural erosion, according to host country governments.

A close examination of the economic, legal, political, and cultural concerns listed in Figure 4–6 indicates that three important trends are emerging. First, data privacy protection laws are being used for economic protectionism. Second, communication costs are rising as the result of the actions taken by the PTTs. Third, as the information-based sector of the world's economy continues to grow, less-developed countries are using informatics policies to close the technology gap between themselves and the rest of the world.

TDF REGULATION BY HOST COUNTRY GOVERNMENTS

Many governments and international quasi-government organizations such as the Organization for Economic and Cultural Development (OECD), the European Commission (EC), and the United Nations (UN) have taken active roles in issues related to transborder data flows. Their efforts, in the form of host country regulations, have focused on two areas: data privacy protection and nonprivacy issues related to national security and national sovereignty.

The Data Privacy Issue and TDFs

Data privacy protection has been a concern of many nation-states since the early 1970s, most notably, in countries such as Sweden and Norway. This concern has led to the implementation of national laws regarding data privacy and transborder data flows. Today, over thirty nations have laws and many more are either considering regulations or are in the process of drafting national laws to control the flow of data across national borders.[7]

There are three contexts in which privacy is an issue: physical, communication, and information.[8] In the physical context, people have a right to privacy in their own homes or domiciles. In the context of communication privacy, conversions or exchanges of information, such as telephone conversations, between two parties are considered private. In the context of information, emphasis is on the collection, storage, processing, and dissemination of information in automated and manual systems for use by record-keeping organizations regarding decision making about individuals by both private and public organizations. Data privacy laws focus specifically on automated systems. Because automated systems can be linked together in other countries through transborder data flows, there is a higher potential for misuse of information about a country's citizens.

In 1978, the French government passed the Data Processing, Data Files, and Individual Liberties Act, which states that "no governmental or private decision may be based solely on automatic processing of data which describes the profile of personality of the person concerned."[9] The threat to TDF is that personal name-linked data can be sent to other countries that do not have similar privacy protection laws or enforcement mechanisms. For example, Swedish authorities are concerned that payroll and personnel data concerning its citizens were being sent to other countries such as the United States for processing and decision making. They were concerned that the information collected, processed, and stored in automated information systems was subject to great misuse and inaccuracy. For example, data supplied by an individual for use in a credit card application may be provided to other organizations for additional uses without the individual's knowledge or consent. As a result, Sweden passed the Data Act of 1973 and established a Data Inspection Board. All private and public organizations must register their databases and are restricted from sending out of the country certain types of data regarding individual citizens.

As one might expect, national laws are not always compatible among different countries. This creates a problem for multinational corporations that operate global information networks. The problem is that each nation's law reflects its own interest, legal system, and compliance mechanism. A national government may not allow data to be sent across its border if the same level of data privacy protection does not exist in the country to which the data is being sent. The problem for the MNC is often not one of local compliance but of compatibility where transborder data flows occur. Data privacy laws vary from country to country with respect to their scope, type of data covered by the regulation, type of data processing system, categories of confidentiality, enforcement mechanisms, and restrictions on cross-border transfers. The legal systems of the host and home countries lead to a problem faced by organizations that operate in many countries—the problem of complying with multiple laws of differing scope and detail. This problem is particularly acute when regulations require the country of destination to have similar data protection laws as the country of origin. The source of the problem is the variety of approaches to enforcement mechanisms used by national governments to implement data privacy protection.

Data Privacy Protection

Figure 4–7 presents a typology of the various government approaches to data privacy protection formulation and enforcement.

Many European governments enact omnibus TDF legislation in which the laws apply to all organizations, both public and private, in all industry sectors. In contrast, the United States takes a sectoral approach, focusing legislation on specific sectors of industry such as banking or insurance. Still other countries rely on international conventions to provide harmonization guidelines such as the ones developed by the OECD, UN, or EC.

Legislation	Enforcement	Approach
Omnibus	Administrative Commission	
		Preventative
Sectoral	Self-Compliance	
		Corrective
International Convention	Code of Ethics and Conduct	

FIGURE 4-7   A Typology of TDF Regulation by Host Country Governments

National data protection laws may also vary significantly in their use of enforcement mechanisms. For example, in Norway an administrative commission has the authority to issue binding regulations or to grant licenses to organizations that collect data in automated systems. In countries such as the United States, enforcement is accomplished through self-compliance and reinforced by judicial action if a violation is detected. A third enforcement mechanism is an enforceable code of ethics and conduct, the primary mechanism used in Great Britain. This mechanism reflects Great Britain's common-law legal system in which specific statutes are not codified as they are in civil-law countries such as the United States.

In summary, national laws take either a preventative or corrective approach. Most European nations emphasize a preventative approach as illustrated through use of database registration and licenses. In contrast, the United States follows a corrective approach, which emphasizes the use of punitive measures such as court action and penalties for violation of the law.

Data privacy laws become a problem for corporations and governments in the host and home countries because of transborder data flows. For example, Sweden does not allow census, payroll, or personnel data to be transmitted to the United States because these types of data do not receive similar treatment under U.S. law. Companies must therefore process and store that data locally in Sweden or in another country with similar privacy protection. Often, the underlying compatibility problem is in each country's application of the law to real persons but not legal persons, as they are defined in the following section.

Legal vs. Real Persons

A *real person* is a citizen. All countries with data privacy laws protect the rights of real people. A *legal person* is an organization such as a corporation. The difference between data privacy protection laws lies in whether or not a legal person is accorded equal protection under the law.

In some European countries such as Denmark, Austria, and Luxembourg, data privacy protection is extended beyond real persons to include legal persons such as professional groups, organizations, corporations, associations, and trade unions. In the United States, Germany, Sweden, France, and many other countries, the concept of a legal person is not included in data privacy laws. Again, we are confronted with the problem of compatibility and reciprocal enforcement when transborder data flows become involved. In addition, the issue of legal versus real persons has other consequences. Countries that favor the recognition of legal persons argue that it is difficult to separate individuals' rights from their business activities. For example, in the case of the small businessperson or entrepreneur, information about the financial situation of the firm cannot be separated from information about the financial situation of the individual. The argument can also be made that large firms may hold an unfair advantage over the small firm because data access rights can be used to distort competition.

Harmonization of Data Privacy Laws

Many groups, including host country governments, have recognized the problem of legal incompatibility and the restrictions that data privacy laws place on transborder data flows. In an effort to harmonize these national laws, organizations such as the EC, the OECD, and the UN have developed data privacy protection principles that national governments use when drafting their laws and regulations.

The United Nations has outlined eleven principles stating the minimum guarantees to be incorporated into national legislation.[10] A summary of these principles follows.

1. *Principle of lawfulness and fairness.* Personal information should be collected or processed in a fair and lawful manner without violating the Charter of the United Nations.

2. *Principle of accuracy.* Persons responsible for collecting and maintaining data and information files have the obligation to ensure its accuracy, relevance, and timeliness.

3. *Principle of purpose-specification.* The purpose for which the file is being created and maintained should be made known to the individual before it is created. Personal data should be approved by the individual and not be maintained beyond the period of time that fulfills the purpose of the file.

4. *Principle of interested-person access.* People have the right to inspect files that contain information about them regardless of their nationality. The cost of correcting any misinformation is the responsibility of the person or organization maintaining the file.

5. *Principle of nondiscrimination.* Information about race, ethnic origin, sex life, political opinions, union or association membership, or religious or other beliefs should not be compiled except as provided in Principle 6, the power to make exceptions.

6. *Power to make exceptions.* Exceptions are provided only in the case of national security, public order, or public health, as provided in a nation's internal law. However, these exceptions are authorized only within the limits of the International Bill of Human Rights.

7. *Principle of security.* Files should be protected against natural dangers, accidental loss or destruction, and unauthorized access.

8. *Supervision and penalties.* Every national law must designate the authority responsible for supervising and enforcing these principles.

9. *Transborder data flows.* The free flow of information between countries cannot be restricted unless there are no reciprocal safeguards provided by each country's legislation.

10. *Field of Application.* These principles apply to both private and public files maintained in computerized and manual systems. They also apply to real persons and legal persons.

11. *Application of the guidelines to personal data files kept by governmental international organizations.* These principles apply to personal data kept by international governmental organization with adjustment made for the differences between internal staff files and external third-party files.

The goal of these principles is to establish a minimum level of privacy protection without restricting the transnational flow of data. Intertwined with data privacy issues are a number of nonprivacy issues that are of great concern to multinational corporations.

Nonprivacy Issues and TDF

By including the concept of a legal person in the data privacy protection laws, the host country governments demonstrate that they are no longer purely motivated by data privacy reasons. The scope and application of these laws begin to shift torward the political and economic dimensions of transborder data flow issues. A former director of France's National Data Processing and Liberties Commission clearly articulated the reason for this shift when he addressed the trade impact of data privacy on transborder data flows and described the power of information to give one country a political and technological advantage over another and, as a result, threaten a nation's security and sovereignty.[11]

Beyond their concern over data privacy protection, national governments have become very aware of their dependence on the data processing and communication industries and the power of information to enhance a country's economic development. The government of the United States is concerned that the use of data privacy laws by some governments will reduce U.S. competition in the information goods and services markets abroad, particularly Europe and Japan. In other words, data privacy laws have been used to encourage the local processing of data, procurement of locally manufactured equipment and software, and employment of native data-processing personnel. The reasons national governments use data privacy laws fall into two categories: national security interests or national sovereignty concerns.

National Security

When sensitive data such as industrial output, research and development data, and government statistics are processed outside a country's national borders there is a degree of vulnerability created by transnational data flows that may affect national security. In 1976, the Nora and Minc report to the French government on the computerization of society described foreign data processing and off-shore databases as having far-reaching effects that could completely change the core of society.[12] Transborder data flows have become a growing national security concern. This concern is reflected in the 1973 International Telecommunications Convention of Málaga-Torremolinas that permits a country to intercept and withhold any communications crossing its borders if that action is in the interest of the country's national security.

Many governments feel that as their economy becomes more information intensive, a loss of control over transborder data flows could lead to disruptions in service from technical breakdowns or work slow-downs in other countries. Transborder data flows also raise control issues for the host government concerning the publication of sensitive information. For example, government-sensitive data, technical information, or economic information may be transmitted out of the country and published or made available through on-line databases. Once the data cross the national border, the national government authorities have no control over its dissemination. If the databases and associated processing reside in the host country, then the government authorities can confiscate or destroy the sensitive data.

National Sovereignty

The world economy is organized through a system of sovereign nations. To claim sovereignty, a nation must be independent; have an effective government capable of conducting foreign relations; and possess a permanent population, an economy, and defined territory.[13] National governments perceive transborder data flows as a threat to national sovereignty because of the potential impact on one or more of the elements used to define national sovereignty. The impact of TDF on national sovereignty may include:

- Television and radio programs originating in one country and broadcast to another that can undermine the cultural values and language of a nation. This is a criticism of American television programs broadcast in Europe and Canada.
- Government regulations in one country affecting the host country. For example, regulations controlling the export of communications and information technology affect the development of the host country telecommunications infrastructure.
- Trade in goods and services that are direct-marketed using videotex technology, creating competition for local producers and advertisers in the host country market.

As the pace of new information technology development accelerates and the accompanying transborder data flows continue to grow, the resulting economic disparity between developed and developing countries will keep the formulation of information policies and regulations an on-going activity of host country governments. While national information policies will enable host countries to more effectively manage the challenges of advancing information technology, the impact will mainly be felt by the managers of multinational corporations who depend on the uninterrupted flow of information across national borders to co-ordinate and control their international activities.

SUMMARY

Transborder data flows are the lifeblood of a multinational corporation's activities. At the same time, they are a potential threat to the national security and sovereignty of the host country because of their role in the development of the nation's information-based economy and their potential impact on the privacy of its citizens. As governments develop new regulations to control the flow of information across national boundaries, multinational corporate managers will continue to seek strategies that enable them to comply with these laws while maintaining the flow of important data and information within the organization.

Successful TDF strategies include reorganization of data processing, use of remote computing services, data reduction, data and systems duplication, and the use of alternative channels. Each of these strategies is designed to address the cost, control, or privacy barriers resulting from TDF regulation.

The development and proliferation of personal computing technology is driving the revision of many TDF regulations and renewing the concerns of host governments. New applications such as telemetry, interactive media, and electronic mail are redefining the nature of TDF in the multinational corporation. More importantly, the new technologies are linking individuals together across national borders. Traditional approaches to TDF regulation by host country governments focused almost exclusively on the organizational level. Future concerns and regulation over privacy and nonprivacy issues of transborder data flows will have to address the individual user as well as the multinational organization.

NOTES

1. D. Farland, "It All Began with Miltiades," *Euromoney* (August 1987): 16.

2. *Transnational Corporations and Transborder Data Flows: A Technical Paper* (New York: United Nations Centre on Transnational Corporations, 1982), 8.

3. There is no accurate figure. See various issues of *Transnational Data and Communication Report* (Washington, DC: Transnational Data Reporting Service, Inc.).

4. *Wall Street Journal*, August 26, 1981, 1.

5. See Steven L. Mandell, *Multinational Corporate Computer-Based Information Systems and the Parent-Subsidiary Interface* (Ph.D. dissertation, George Washington University, 1975).

6. *Telecommunications and Canada* (Ottawa, Canada: Consultative Committee on the Implications for Canadian Sovereignty, Information Canada, 1979), 16.

7. See *Transnational Data and Communications Report* (Washington, DC: Transnational Data Reporting Service, Inc.) for current status of country legislation.

8. *Transnational Data Flows: Concerns in Privacy Protection and Free Flow of Information* (Washington, DC: American Federation of Information Processing Societies Panel on Transborder Data Flow, 1979), 57.

9. *Data Processing, Data Files, and Individual Liberties Act*, Act 78–17, Paris, France, January 6, 1978.

10. "UN Guidelines Concerning Computerized Personal Data Files," *Transnational Data and Communication Report* (Washington, DC: Transnational Data Reporting Service, Inc., November 1989), 35–36.

11. Speech in Geneva, Switzerland, 1978.

12. S. Nora and A. Minc, *Report on the Computerization of Society* (Paris, France: Board of Financial Examiners, 1976).

13. Litka, Michael, *International Dimensions of the Legal Environment of Business* (Boston: PWS-Kent Publishing Company, 1988), 11.

STUDY QUESTIONS

1. Who are the key actors in the debate over transborder data flow regulation? What are their key concerns?

2. Briefly describe the major strategies used by multinational corporations to address the impact of TDF regulation.

3. Are multinational service firms such as banks and trading companies more affected than manufacturing enterprises are by TDF regulation? Explain.

4. Why do host country governments have concerns over data privacy issues related to transborder data flows?

5. Why is data privacy protection often perceived as an economic issue by host country governments?

SUGGESTED READINGS

Ajami, R. "Global Transborder Data Flows: Concerns and Options." *International Journal of Technology Management* 5 (1991): 589–604.

Basche, James R. *Regulating International Data Transmission: The Impact of Managing International Business.* New York: The Conference Board, 1984.

Beavois, John J. "International Intelligence for International Enterprise." *California Management Review* 3(2) (1961): 39–46.

Business International. "Multinational Corporations are Depending on Data Flows—Results of a BI Survey." *Business International* (August 8, 1983).

Buss, Martin D. J. "Legislative Threat to Transborder Data Flow." *Harvard Business Review* (March–April 1984): 111–118.

Carper, William B. "Transborder Data Flows in the Information Age: Implications for International Management." *International Journal of Management* (December 1989): 418–425.

Chandran, Rajan, Arvind Phatak, and Rakesh Sambharya. "Transborder Data Flows: Implications for Multinational Corporations." *Business Horizons* (November/December 1987): 74–82.

Diebold, John. "The Problem of Moving Data Across National Borders." *Management Review* (July 1980): 29–30.

Fishman, William. "Introduction to Transborder Data Flow." *Stanford Journal of International Law* (Summer 1980): 9–10.

Grub, Philip, and Suzanne R. Settle. "Transborder Data Flows: An Endangered Species." In *The Multinational Enterprise in Transition*, 2nd ed., edited by Philip Grub et al., Princeton, NJ: Darwin Press, 1984.

Guynes, J. L. "The Impact of Transborder Data Flow Regulation." *Journal of Information Systems Management* (Summer 1990): 70–73.

Kane, Michael J., and David A. Ricks. "Is Transnational Data Flow a Real Problem?" *Journal of International Business Studies* (Fall 1988): 477–482.

Kane, Michael J., and David A. Ricks. "The Impact of Transborder Data Flow Regulation on Large U.S.-Based Multinational Corporations." *Columbia Journal of World Business* (Summer 1989): 23–29.

Little, Arthur D. *Impact: The Regulation of Transnational Data Flow.* Boston: Arthur D. Little Decision Resource, 1981.

Samiee, Saeed. "Developments in Transnational Data Flows: Regulations and Perspectives." *Journal of International Business Studies* (Winter 1983): 159–162.

Samiee, Saeed. "Transnational Data Flow Constraints: A New Challenge to Multinational Corporations." *Journal of International Business Studies* (Spring 1984): 141–150.

Chapter FIVE

INTERNATIONAL TELECOMMUNICATIONS AND GLOBAL CONNECTIVITY

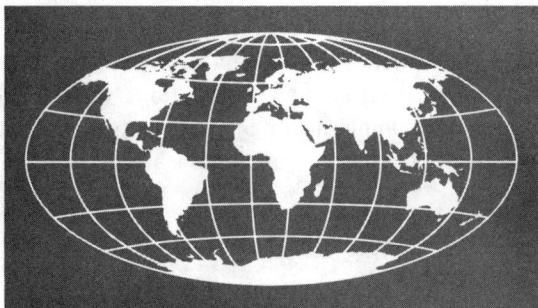

The global communications infrastructure provides the information linkage necessary for multinational corporations to sustain their world-wide operations. Today, many industries such as the airlines and financial institutions rely heavily on connections to a global information network. For these firms, the global business day never ends. In recent years, a global loop has developed that is geared to financial markets and tied together by the dollar.[1] The eighteen-hour time spread between the financial capitals of the Far East, the United States, and Western Europe add further complexity to existing systems.[2] With greater demands on the world's communications networks, MNCs may face an array of complexities depending upon whether they operate in the developed or developing world. Globally, telecommunications restrictions are more stringent than they are in the United States, and they can be a major problem in developing countries. It has become increasingly important for IS managers in multinational corporations to keep abreast of telecommunications developments around the world. Networking and communications management are receiving top priority as corporations strive to take full advantage of the changes and advancements in communications technology. Successful MNCs are recognizing the importance of linking their business strategy to an international technology strategy.[3] It has become necessary for the firm to have its telecommunications infrastructure in place before other technologies can be used to optimal strategic advantage.[4] Telecommunications standards, regulations, and policies will clearly influence the firm's ability to compete successfully in a global marketplace.

In this chapter we will discuss in more detail important issues relevant to implementing and managing the firm's telecommunications on an international scale. Issues specific to the global integration of technologies and resulting international applications will be incorporated. The importance of telecommunications as the infrastructure and facilitator of global business cannot be overemphasized.

INTERNATIONAL TELECOMMUNICATIONS

Telecommunications involves the transmission or reception of signals, writings, sounds, images, or any form of information through wire, fiber optics, satellite links, or other electromagnetic systems. Connections may be within a building, across a state or country, or international through telephone companies or private facilities. When operating in the international environment, companies may encounter complications not normally met in the domestic (U.S.) operating environment. In some countries, for example, firms may be required to use a worldwide standard modem rather than their usual brand of modem.[5] The decision-making variables for a strictly domestic (U.S.) decision are often not the most appropriate for a similar decision in another country. For example, a company with much international data traffic may wish to install its own satellite station. This decision may not be a simple make-versus-buy or leased-line-versus-satellite-cost decision as it would be in the United States. In many countries, where the PTT owns the antenna and support equipment, a rental agreement would need to be arranged.[6]

International leased lines, in which leased lines are reserved for the private use of the leasing customer, are mandatory for most multinational corporations. American Express, for example, services approximately 250,000 requests daily with a five-second response time. This response would not be possible with a public switched network, in which a shared line requires a connection to be made each time by dialing.[7] To obtain an international line, a firm must submit an application similar to that required for a national leased line. Two monthly statements are received, one in the country in which the request is initiated and the other in the country in which the line is terminated. Negotiations take place between PTTs at each end. When intermediate countries are involved, negotiations are worked out by the PTT that initiates the request.[8] These constraints are further complicated by the multiplicity of countries involved. The importance of telecommunications is well understood in most developed countries and efforts are underway to improve the available telecommunications infrastructure. In many less-developed countries, however, even base services, such as telephones, are not available and newer technologies are years away.

Today, telecommunications are strategic to every nation's progress. Governments are well aware of the economic benefits afforded by an adequate information network.[9] Telecommunications sophistication varies considerably from one country to another. Business expansion to Eastern Europe, Latin America and the Pacific Rim will require companies to make adjustments in their expectations of telecommunications. The Eastern European nations, for example, do not have anything close to a modern telecommunications infrastructure.[10] There is no question that telecommunications are of major importance for both users and manufacturers of telecommunications as worldwide business expansion demands connectivity.

The trend in many corporations today is to link communications planning more closely with corporate strategy. As corporations depend more and more on communications for timely and accurate information flows to support their key business objectives, the distinction between the firm's telecommunications and information systems becomes more blurred. Today, the IS executive must be well versed in telecommunications. Multinationals are increasingly bringing together information systems and telecommunications under the IS manager who understands the business dimension.[11] Today, a corporation survives or dies based on its ability to communicate locally as well as globally.[12]

International Standards

Standardization has become an increasingly important concern for international telecommunications. Standards include rules for connecting equipment and communication procedures at the most minute level of detail. As telecommunications becomes even more vital to the nationwide and worldwide success of the organization, pressures to speed development will hinge on successful establishment of global standards for connectivity.[13] Standards will be one of the major economic and political issues of the 1990s.[14] International cooperation has taken on added significance as pressures build for worldwide organizations to reach agreements on international standards that permit interconnections of national networks across national borders.[15] The global, telecommunications-information standards-making process has reached a critical state and represents a several-hundred-million-dollar-a-year undertaking. Standards making has become the dominant activity in the telecommunications-information world today.[16]

As corporate managers of voice, data, and image communications put together networks that are manageable and cost effective across various countries, they are continually faced with a maze of standards that present obstacles to the effective implementation of these systems. The continual series of debates in the standards-setting process slows progress. Multinationals—not international committees, vendors, or PTTs—set the pace for international standards. The electronic consortium of banks known as SWIFT is an example of firms that have banded together to force system standards to be developed. Better competition can be achieved through cooperation in establishing a shared standard.[17] It is imperative that global communications depend on universal, not regional or local, standards.[18] It has become increasingly important for IS managers to participate in user groups and standards organizations in order to air their concerns.

Standards organizations will play a significant role in the future direction of international telecommunications. Generally, standards are developed by committees consisting of representatives from leading companies in an industry. In the United States, the American National Standards Institute (ANSI) is the umbrella organization for all other standards organizations.[19] Most standards developed by U.S. organizations are recommendations, whereas in other countries, telecommunications are regulated by postal, telephone, and telegraph companies, which usually impose strict requirements on communications equipment.

The two major international standards organizations are the Consultative Committee on International Telephone and Telegraph (CCITT) and the International Standards Organization (ISO). The CCITT membership consists of regulating bodies from member countries, representatives from other organizations, and company leaders in telecommunications. In the ISO, member countries are represented by their own national standards organization. Although these two organizations cooperate on some standards, they generally operate independently. They may develop different standards for the same technical areas.[20]

There are many regional, national, and international standards organizations that address the issues at various network planning and standards forums worldwide. One of the more prominent organizations is the International Telecommunication Union (ITU), which plays a major role in international cooperation in the planning and use of all kinds of telecommunications. Specifically, the significant functions of the ITU include: (1) encouraging global consensus, (2) providing an open exchange of information, (3) facilitating network development, and (4) providing leadership for a global networked environment.[21]

On an international scale, the Consultative Committee on International Telephone and Telegraph (CCITT) and the International Radio Consultative Committee (CCIR) play significant roles through their work with regional standards bodies and high-priority, market-driven concerns. The work for these bodies has become increasingly difficult and it has become a formidable task to respond quickly enough to the dynamic demands and standards needs of an information-dependent society.[22]

In an effort to more quickly address market-driven needs, key standards-setting bodies from the Unites States, Europe, and Japan met in 1990 for what has been recognized as one of the most significant international standards conferences to date, and in which they took a positive, proactive stance in laying the groundwork for future developments. Participants included the U.S.A. Committee T1, the European Telecommunications Standards Institute (ETSI), and Japan's Telecommunications Technology Committee (TTC). This group established guidelines that have become known as the Fredericksburg Plan (the meeting was held in Fredericksburg, Virginia). Major components of the plan include the following provisions.[23]

1. International standards should be a managed process and respond to market requirements.

2. Standardization projects should have a defined scope and date for delivery.

3. Better cooperation between regional and national standards bodies will help identify the most important standardization priorities.

4. Standards bodies should continue to meet at regular intervals to discuss progress in global standards developments.

5. Agreements to exchange documents, ideas, and so on about worldwide standards at an early stage of development and on an informal basis would avoid delays in the formal process.

This meeting represents a step toward addressing the pressing concerns initiated by market demands. To further emphasize the importance of global telecommunications, conferences of other major organizations are, likewise, addressing the needs of those responsible for corporate communications. These needs have become increasingly significant as responsibilities of telecommunications managers have grown from geographic regions to global arenas in the 1990s.[24]

On a more limited scale, numerous standards-making bodies address issues specific to a particular technology or interface. For example, international protocol standards are of significance to the advancement of telecommunications internationally. In simple terms, a communications protocol is a set of hardware and software standards designed for transmitting data between terminals and computers. On an international level, lack of standards creates greater complexity in setting up communications networks to support the firm's business activities.

Postal, Telephone, and Telegraph Companies (PTTs)

In international telecommunications, an important concern centers on regulatory strategies imposed by the postal, telephone, and telegraph (PTT) companies in other countries. In the United States, deregulation of the telephone companies (Telcos) has become a reality. In other countries, the PTTs are usually monopolies and may be the largest employer in the country. Regulations, procedures, and tariff structures may vary considerably from one country to another.[25] Dealing with the PTTs is unique to operating in the international business environment and not an issue for the strictly domestic U.S. firm.

PTTs are operating entities or government administrations that may oversee a nation's entire communications and transportation infrastructure from telephones to railroads. In regulating the flow of information, they are in effect gatekeepers to national markets. The PTTs are also closely tied to the country's social, political, and economic institutions. Revenues generated by the PTT may, for example, be used to fund social programs. Government subsidization of the PTT is common in many countries.[26]

Two basic reasons for establishing regulatory strategies include revenue generation and protection. For foreign MNCs, regulatory strategies imposed by PTTs cause the most concern. Attempting to protect the national markets, the PTTs make it difficult to transfer data and information in a cost-effective manner. They make it more difficult for foreign MNCs to compete in their markets. Artificially higher telecommunications costs may affect long-term planning. A common concern is poorer quality service, which results from being revenue oriented rather than service oriented.[27]

The PTTs control many things. In some countries, regulations prohibit companies from setting up their own networks and require that lines be leased from the PTT. To discourage the use of private lines that are in direct competition with the PTTs, companies may not be allowed to attach equipment such as concentrators or nodes to lines linked to centers in other countries. Regulations may also prohibit foreign MNCs from using products other than those produced locally. PTTs may also practice regulation through foot-dragging. for example, taking years to give approval for a phone line. They may also refuse requests to import equipment that is impossible to obtain locally, or refuse to approve equipment that is not compatible with foreign networks. For example, the United States and Canada use standards developed by AT&T, whereas other countries adhere to standards imposed by the International Telegraph and Telephone Consultative Committee.

PTT monopolies are also responsible for developing and controlling the use of new systems. Regulations may be imposed that cause hardships and tremendous overhead for companies that have set up their systems using American-made hardware and software. Companies need a choice of network services for flexibility in setting up systems to meet their individual needs.

For MNCs operating in several countries, the challenges become even more complex. PTT regulations vary considerably from country to country and change constantly. In the global scheme, it is a tremendous task to avoid violating regulations. PTTs are also highly influenced by politics; a new government can create major changes in regulations.

PTT regulations may have serious consequences for MNCs operating in PTT-regulated countries. In comparing the U.S. telephone companies with the PTT, two issues are key to understanding the challenges facing the U.S.-based IS executive. The first issue is structure. In the United States, the telephone companies are privately owned and revenues go back to the companies. The PTTs are government owned and revenues serve the interests of the government. The second issue is competition. U.S. telephone companies are competitive and, therefore, necessarily service oriented. Because PTTs are monopolies, they place less emphasis on customer needs and, as a result, service quality may lag behind.

Actions of the PTT have far reaching implications for future directions of international telecommunications. There is a real concern that PTTs restrict the growth of telecommunications because planning is more difficult and, at the same time, less economical. International standards would greatly simplify the existing complexity associated with the establishment of communication networks to support the firm's international operations. Likewise, the eventual success of new technologies such as Integrated Services Digital Networks (ISDN) may also be affected by actions taken by the PTT. For some companies, a solution is to set up plants only in countries where an American telecommunications company such as IBM or AT&T is already established. This strategy makes it easier to abide by strict regulatory laws and still get the necessary services. When setting up operations in a new country, it is important to establish relationships with the PTT. It is of utmost importance to be prepared to deal with the PTT, and in some cases companies have hired experts to deal exclusively with these monopolies.

Price and Quality of Telecommunications Support

Directly linked to the PTT issue, price and quality of telecommunications support from one country to another is an important consideration for firms operating in many different countries. Inconveniences associated with long lead times for line availability, terminals, or other necessary equipment can become significant. Differences in the available technological infrastructures from one country to another may pose particular obstacles for companies setting up multicountry networks. Private networks that span several countries are pieced together using tariff services of the telephone companies in each country of operation. Multinationals spend much time negotiating tariffs and providing for connections across borders. Yet, services often do not match from one country to another.[28] Because the telecommunications environment is complex, it is necessary to be well informed and to compare prices. There may be substantial variations in cost, tariffs, and regulations from country to country. Tariff structures continually change as countries move toward more liberal telecommunications. In some parts of the world such as Africa, services are difficult to obtain, if they are available at all. It may be necessary to settle for less than one would like in some parts of the world. In most countries, network services are provided by only one carrier. In some industrialized countries, however, competing international services are expected in the near future. There is currently some movement toward cooperation among carriers in different countries. Carrier cooperation will help reduce the complexity associated with managing international networks.[29]

Value Added Network Services (VANs)

As international information flows increase, the use of value added network services (VANs) will likely gain increased attention in the international context. Beyond normal transmission, a VAN provides additional services such as protocol conversion, facsimile interfacing, or conference calls. For the medium-to-small-sized company, VANs may offer reliability and additional benefits not available or affordable through private networks. With a minimal capital investment, the company will have access to more powerful computer systems, larger databases, and specialized software supported by a professional staff.[30] Larger companies with substantial international involvement may have the resources to set up their own private international networks. However, even these companies are not without problems. A technical staff is usually required to work with each national PTT. There may be little transfer of technical knowledge among local personnel from one country to another. There are substantial tradeoffs and many dimensions to consider.[31]

Depending upon the country involved, VANs may be provided only by the PTT, only by private companies, or by both PTTs and private companies.[32] In many countries, PTTs have been hesitant to open their networks to value added service suppliers. A major reason for their concern is the potential loss of control of high-value services, reducing their role to simply providing commodity transmission.[33]

Integrated Services Digital Network (ISDN)

ISDN is another issue of particular significance for international tele-communications and has become an important topic of discussion within the last few years. ISDN involves the ability to send and receive voice, data, text, and image signals simultaneously over a totally digital net-work. To the user, ISDN is an all-purpose plug that is capable of accepting telephone, computer, facsimile, and video. One ISDN line replaces the separate lines for each device, making it possible to send and receive all types of information. The aim of ISDN is to provide a world communication system that will meet the needs of the information age.[34] To accomplish this goal, standards will play a big part. International consensus is strong that the question today is not whether ISDN will proceed, but how.

Although ISDN technology has significant implications for international telecommunications, there is much controversy concerning the evolution of the technology for domestic and international business. Much of the controversy involves coordinating the international aspects. This means adopting standards, but for competitive reasons, many vendors are slow to move in this direction.[35]

It is strongly believed that during the next decade, ISDN will evolve as the dominant technology for worldwide data and voice communications. ISDN is being recognized as the means by which globally competing international firms can establish a comprehensive telecommunications strategy. ISDN provides a cost-effective means by which to support the overall business plan. Furthermore, ISDN opens up opportunities for profitable business operations that otherwise would not be possible in many small countries.[36]

Every major company in the world will have to make a decision about ISDN in the near future. In fact, purchase decisions that are made today may delay the firm's entry into ISDN, while competitors that enter into ISDN now may gain an advantage.[37] On an international scale, ISDN provides the business an opportunity to establish a complete global communications network. To remain competitive, ISDN offers tremendous advantages for overcoming many of the obstacles of operating on an international scale. Of course, there will be problems because ISDN has the potential to cut across a nation's political, social, and economic boundaries, barriers which do not fall easily.[38] Political obstacles, engineering considerations, and vendor benefits will play a significant role in the eventual acceptance or delay in the implementation of ISDN.[39]

Despite these concerns, ISDN represents the potential vehicle for businesses to build a global information highway.

Standards and technological support for ISDN are complex. Currently, U.S. telephone companies cannot agree on standards for nationwide ISDN. It is expected that events such as those anticipated by the economic integration of twelve European nations by the end of 1992 will bring with them a push for nationwide connectivity in the United States. Even though there remains controversy concerning ISDN, implementation of international standards to support the technology, and problems of implementation in many parts of the world, there appears to be no question that ISDN is coming in some form. Other parts of the world including Japan, Europe, and Canada are making considerable strides with the technology.[40] ISDN represents an evolving worldwide strategic opportunity.[41]

Telecommunications Deregulation

It is expected that through the year 2000, there will be a continuing decline in the regulation of telecommunications in the United States. Outside the United States, telecommunications policies are, likewise, expected to be substantially liberalized. On an international scale, the degree of telecommunications liberalization is expected to be highly correlated to the degree of economic development. It is anticipated that developed countries such as Great Britain and Japan will move toward liberalized policies; less-developed countries will continue to enforce service regulations but will allow competition in equipment markets; and newly industrialized countries will likely remain protected for a long period of time.[42]

These declines in regulations will certainly have significant business implications. As telecommunications is increasingly vulnerable to market forces, fundamental changes will be needed.[43] The firm's strategies must be consistent with the current situation. In a regulatory environment, emphasis will be on universal service and pricing. In a deregulated environment, emphasis will be shifted to the needs of the end users. Regulatory considerations can then be factored in as appropriate.[44]

In an international context, the resolution of regulatory conflicts and the scope and nature of resulting regulatory definitions will vary by country and change over time. For MNCs, the problem centers on how the firm might best compete in this transitional environment. Clearly, the decline in regulations will not be smooth or predictable.[45]

INTEGRATION OF TECHNOLOGIES

Integration of technologies (for example, data processing, telecommunications, and office automation) has taken on increased significance for the effective use of information technology resources. The proliferation of products and vendors and rapid changes in telecommunications technology make integration of technology more difficult, especially in the context of the firm's international business operations. There is clearly an increasingly heightened interest in the integration of hardware, software, workstations, and telecommunications. As the market moves toward integration, telecommunications has taken on an increasingly significant role in the overall plans and operations of the corporation. [46] MNCs are looking to information technology as a critical element in their quest for gaining and maintaining a competitive edge in a rapidly changing marketplace. The United States' competitive position in the world market will depend on the firm's effective use and innovative application of information technology. [47] Operating in a multivendor, multicountry, and multitechnology world creates obstacles and challenges for those in leadership positions to make the critical decisions affecting international telecommunications.

Global Network Management

As global networks grow and become more sophisticated, increased emphasis will be placed on the effective management of this tremendous resource. Once the business begins to rely on electronic delivery on a large scale, it will in turn begin to depend on the availability and reliability of its telecommunications network with the same urgency that it depends on the electrical utility. [48] When the network goes down, the business goes down as well. Depending upon the nature of the firm's business, this downtime can have a substantial economic impact. The critical issue is no longer the size of the network itself, but rather the value and importance of the information that the network carries. [49]

It is expected that by the year 2000, there will be a major shift in the way people think about using networks. [50] Networks will provide the communication backbone for the exchange of data and information. Clearly, network management will become an increasingly important issue in the decade ahead.

The issue of network management standards will receive increased attention as agreements evolve over time. Currently, network standards are difficult to define since, to a large degree, no standards exist. An analogy can be made between network management protocols and voltage standards. An American 110-volt appliance can work with a European 220-volt appliance through use of a converter, but the appliance may not be as convenient to use or as effective. Incompatible network protocols can be made to communicate, but the process is more complex.[51]

At some point, companies must decide which standard to adopt for their networks.[52] Presently, the two leading standards are the Systems Network Architecture (SNA) supported by IBM and the Open Systems Interconnect (OSI) model supported by the International Standards Organization (ISO). The technical details of these models are complex; it is necessary here to discuss only the significance of these developments for international telecommunications. The OSI model is a worldwide standard the primary purpose of which is to prevent users from becoming dependent on proprietary vendor network architectures. Development of the OSI model as a flexible and multivendor network system began in 1977 and the base-level OSI is currently in the first phase of implementation. The open architecture of the OSI model represents a step toward international consensus and many recognize it as *the* global network architecture.[53] IBM's SNA model, on the other hand, is a proprietary architecture. There is current debate that those organizations sticking with proprietary models such as SNA will eventually fall behind in their ability to compete as the OSI networks offer superior performance in the future. On the other side of the debate, there are those who feel that IBM will provide good network management solutions for tomorrow. IBM is committed to making their solutions a success.[54] How these issues unfold and what directions companies take remain to be seen.

The ISDN concept is closely linked with standards for computers to communicate. ISDN has standards for interpreting communication protocols through the use of the OSI model. Based on this concept, a message spoken in French can be sent over an ISDN phone and be heard in English in the United States.[55]

A strategy known as Virtual Private Network (VPN) is coming of age and receiving increased attention. This strategy involves contracting for services and telecommunications services, thereby leaving network management to the experts. The VPN provides the fixed cost benefits of a private network without the major capital investments in hardware and in-house staff to run the network. For many reasons, there are many advantages to the VPNs. Among the more important are: (1) network management is much more complex, (2) global network topologies require linkages over lines that vary in quality and require around-the-clock management in various countries, and (3) domestic experience in network management is not easily transferable outside the United States due to country-specific differences in procedures and telecommunications infrastructures. Even through cost-justification for them may be more complex, global VPNs are expected to grow at a rapid rate in the 1990s.[56]

Vendor Selection and Support

In facilitating the firm's efforts toward integrating its various technologies, vendor support in foreign subsidiaries may be an important factor. In the foreign operating environment, the size of the local market may dictate the number of available vendors as well as the quality of service that is provided. Vendors of information technology products and services are quick to try to convince companies that they have the answers to all the firm's technological needs, from PCs to workstations to networks.[57]

For MNCs that develop a comprehensive international technology strategy, the choice of vendors will be guided by vendor support. In a multivendor environment, most MNCs are refusing to lock into one vendor for all their needs. The trend is to build alliances with a variety of suppliers. It is no longer considered a good strategy to depend on a single vendor or dominant-vendor plan of action.[58] It is unrealistic to assume that any one supplier could provide all the equipment for MNCs that operate a large communications network. The firm's flexibility in making vendor decisions on a global scale will likely depend on the location of the firm's international business operations.

It is felt that future successful vendors will be those that recognize the importance of working with users at the strategic level to integrate products and technical know-how with business strategy. This dimension will require expertise in business and integration. Vendors that demonstrate this ability will be recognized as having the real added value. It is clear that the role of the vendor is moving from one of selling products toward one of managing a customer relationship.[59]

Data Security

Data security is an issue relevant to the firm's effective integration of technology, especially on an international scale. Balance of data availability, accessibility, and security can be complex in the international arena. When users are allowed access to data terminals or telephone lines, there is an implication of risk for the data involved.[60]

Security issues are of particular concern for financial institutions that move large amounts of money by electronic means; money is exchanged, even though it is traveling in digital form.[61] Network security is another area that will receive increased attention as access to a network proliferates. With enhanced vulnerability, greater security measures will be mandatory.[62]

Carriers claim they can provide the level of security required by including fingerprint and voice identification, if the customer is willing to pay the price. Those providing security systems will have many issues to consider. Individual security strategies for users of sensitive data[63] will evolve along with other advancements in telecommunications and information technology.

End-User Computing

Because users will play an increasingly important role in the development of telecommunications applications and the successful integration of technologies, end-user computing is a rapidly growing area in many organizations. Although international end-user computing problems are much the same as they are domestically, firms tend to lag behind in adopting new technology internationally. International implementation of IS technology is often simply a fallout of what has worked domestically. Internationally, control and communication may pose particular problems with data integrity, data ownership, maintenance of files, and backup. If end-user computing is not managed, there is the danger, for example, that various databases may be developed that generate many different reports. If reporting is delayed as long as a month and exchange rates change, particular problems could arise in highly inflationary countries.

IS executives view the United States as a larger, more homogeneous, and more mainframe-oriented market. Europe is more mini- and PC-based. Some executives foresee end-user computing as the only economic tool for automation in small countries (for example, using the PC-based system as a simple tool). Users will likely play a significant role in the applications-driven needs for telecommunications capabilities. This will, in turn, exert pressure on vendors to respond to these growing market demands.[64]

INTERNATIONAL APPLICATIONS

International advancements in telecommunications technology will provide MNCs with capabilities and applications never before possible. Telecommunications presently provides greater international communication capabilities such as electronic mail, videotex, and teleconferencing. International integration of these technologies to meet the needs of the business will not be an easy task. On a global scale, the challenge is to achieve connectivity that allows these individual technologies maximum potential for intercommunication.

Interorganizational Systems

Interorganizational systems facilitate the flow of information across organizational boundaries. These systems may be competitive or cooperative. Strategic systems achieve competitive advantage by surprising the firm's competitors. These systems *may* by interorganizational, but cooperative systems *must* be interorganizational. Generally, the term *interorganizational system* refers to the cooperative system.[65]

Interorganizational systems require at least two parties to collaborate on the development of a joint, computer-based system.[66] By participating in the system, each firm benefits in some capacity and achieves competitive advantage.[67] These systems are getting increased attention as multinational firms more seriously consider partnerships and alliances to overcome some of the obstacles of operating in the international arena. One form of interorganizational system receiving increased attention is Electronic Data Interchange (EDI).

Electronic Data Interchange (EDI)

EDI is the electronic transmission of data from a computer application in one business to a computer application in another business.[68] The emphasis is on direct electronic communication that provides a substitute for paper document transfer. EDI has the potential to streamline operations, improve cash flow, and reduce inventory. Proper implementation of this technology requires careful, up-front planning and organization. It is necessary to establish physical connections between computers as well as assure a format that allows accurate, timely, and useful transmission of information.[69] EDI is distinguished from other electronic means of communication such as electronic mail by the necessity for prearranged agreements on standards and applications between business partners.[70]

EDI technology has tremendous implications for the firm's international operations. As with other technologies discussed previously, most of the problems, both domestic and international, center on the lack of standards. Worldwide, there are a variety of standards organizations and other associations working together for consolidation and cooperation on standards agreements.[71] The proliferation of competing standards has hindered large-scale acceptance of EDI applications. Internationally, agreement on a common standard would likely require some modification of two prominent competing standards. An international user's association has been developed for the purpose of addressing the EDI issue for use with administrative and trade data worldwide.[72]

In some industries, the use of a third-party network for EDI has been successful. The MOTORNET network in Europe is an example of a system linking suppliers and manufacturers in the auto industry. SWIFT is an example of a cooperatively owned international network of over 2,000 banks worldwide. VANs also provide transmission links for companies wishing to implement EDI.[73] This technology will certainly have tremendous potential as telecommunications becomes more sophisticated and less complex worldwide.

Global Decision Support Systems

Systems for decision support can be extended to incorporate the multitude of uncertain, unstructured, and complex decisions of a world marketplace. For companies striving to achieve a global strategic plan for information technology, decision support systems capable of integrating extensive databases and models provide the potential for enhanced decision-making opportunities.[74] Enhanced telecommunications will play a key role in the successful development of these systems by moving the firm from individual decision-making tasks to group- and organizationwide decision making.[75] Telecommunications provides the means by which to move from small-scale systems to systems that can improve organizational productivity on a global scale. Of course, there is still much progress to be made in the global context.

One area offering much telecommunications potential is that of executive information systems (EIS). These systems can collect decentralized, geographically dispersed data for immediate management attention. There will also likely be an enhanced emphasis on the integration of information systems such as marketing information systems and accounting information systems, which are specific to the firm's subfunctions. The telecommunications infrastructure will provide the support base for application developments in these areas.

SUMMARY

Globalization of telecommunications and connectivity to support global expansion has been described by key executives in the field as the most important issue for the coming decade. Telecommunications will provide the infrastructure for the information age. As firms become increasingly dependent on the transfer, use, and management of information technology on a worldwide scale, telecommunications issues will receive top-priority attention.[76] International business trends are forcing major corporations to become better informed about the changes and developments in telecommunications. Global connectivity will provide the means by which to support the firm's global business strategy.[77]

It is impossible to discuss all the aspects of telecommunications that are currently evolving and likely to eventually affect the global operations of MNCs. By the time this book is published, more changes will have occurred. There will be an uneven rate of change in telecommunications developments throughout the world. We have provided an overview of the important considerations. The need for international standards and the increased emphasis on global telecommunications issues can only be expected to grow. The telecommunications environment will continue to evolve as we progress in this information age.

NOTES

1. Peter Cowhey, "The Globalization of Telephone Pricing and Services," *Telecommunications* (January 1988): 39.
2. Dennis W. Elliott, "North Pacific Cable Meets Asian Connectivity Needs," *Telecommunications* (February 1990): 39.
3. Peter G. W. Keen and Martha M. Ruh, "The New Vendor/Customer Alliance: Surviving a Shakeout in the Multi-Vendor, Multi-Technology World," International Center for Information Technology briefing paper (Washington, D.C., 1989), 3.
4. Ibid., 7.
5. Walter L. Vignault, *Worldwide Telecommunications Guide for the Business Manager* (New York: John Wiley & Sons, Inc., 1987), 9.

6. Ibid.

7. Ibid., 46.

8. Ibid.

9. William Bazzy, "Strategic Telecommunications," *Telecommunications Business* (April 1989): 5–7.

10. Alexander E. Braun, "The ICA Conference and Exposition: Preparing for the 90s," *Telecommunications* (May 1990): 91.

11. Keen and Ruh, 7.

12. Braun, 86.

13. Richard E. Butler, "The Changing Environment: Multidimensional Issues," *Telecommunications Policy* (August 1990): 275.

14. Ibid. 278.

15. R. E. Butler, "The Role of the ITU in Global Telecommunications," *Telecommunications* (August 1987): 33.

16. Pekka J. Tarjanne, "Open Frameworks for Telecommunications in the 1990s: Access to Networks and Markets," *Telecommunications* (April 1990): 23.

17. Keen and Ruh, 9.

18. J. David Sulser, "The Business Meaning of Integrated Services Digital Networks: Unmasking Political ISDN to Reveal User's ISDN," International Center for Information Technology briefing paper (Washington, D.C., 1989), 11.

19. William J. Beyda, *Basic Data Communications* (New Jersey: Prentice Hall, Inc., 1989), 51.

20. Ibid., 52

21. Tarjanne, 24.

22. James N. Budwey, "Interregional Summit on Telecommunications Standards," *Telecommunications* (April 1990): 25.

23. Tarjanne, 26.

24. Braun, 86.

25. Vignault, 8.

26. Ibid.

27. Gary Stix, "PTTs Make Life Rough Overseas," *Computer Decisions* (April 9, 1985): 122.

28. Janet Fiderio, "Information Must Conform In a World Without Borders," *Computerworld* (October 1, 1990): 100.

29. Ibid.

30. Vignault, 255.
31. Ibid., 256.
32. Ibid., 254.
33. David E. Harper, "The Future of Telecommunications: Part II," *Telecommunications* (February 1989): 49.
34. Sulser, 3.
35. James F. Donohue, "Exploding Five Myths About ISDN," *Mini-Micro Systems* (March 1988): 33.
36. Sulser, 1.
37. Ibid.
38. Ibid, 2.
39. Ibid., 3.
40. Donohue, 34.
41. Sulser, 4.
42. David E. Harper, "The Future of Telecommunications: Part I," *Telecommunications* (January 1989): 31.
43. Ibid., 31.
44. Ibid., 32.
45. Ibid., 33.
46. Keen and Ruh, 6.
47. Ibid., 1.
48. Sharlene Sue, "Network Management: An Executive Overview," International Center for Information Technology briefing paper (Washington, D.C., 1987), 1.
49. Ibid., 2.
50. Harper, 30.
51. Sue, 5.
52. Ibid., 6.
53. Sulser, 12.
54. Sue, 8.
55. Sulser, 4.
56. James D. Heerwagen, "Global Virtual Private Networks," *Telecommunications* (November 1990): 49.
57. Keen and Ruh, 2.
58. Ibid.
59. Ibid., 7.

60. Sulser, 13.

61. Sulser, 12.

62. Braun, 91.

63. Sulser, 13.

64. Harper, 54.

65. Barbara C. McNurlin and Ralph H. Sprague, Jr., *Information Systems Management in Practice*, 2nd ed. (New Jersey: Prentice Hall, Inc., 1989), 71.

66. Ibid.

67. Raymond McLeod, Jr., *Management Information Systems* (New York: Macmillian, 1990, 708.

68. John Dearing, "The Strategic Benefits of EDI," *The Journal of Business Strategy* (January/February 1990): 4.

69. Daniel W. Edwards, "Electronic Data Interchange: A Senior Management Overview," International Center for Information Technology briefing paper (Washington, D.C., 1987), 1.

70. Ibid., 2.

71. Ibid., 4.

72. Ibid., 5.

73. Ibid., 6.

74. Raja K. Iyer, "Information and Modeling Resources for Decision Support in Global Environments," *Information and Management* (February 1988): 67.

75. Peter G. W. Keen, "Decision Support Systems: The Next Decade," International Center for Information Technology briefing paper (Washington, D.C., 1987), 14.

76. Harper, 27.

77. Keen and Ruh, 10.

STUDY QUESTIONS

1. Explain the role of standards organizations in addressing market demands for international telecommunications standards.

2. What is the role of postal, telephone, and telegraph (PTT) companies in other countries? How do these companies differ from the telephone companies in the United States.?

3. Discuss the implications of ISDN technology for the future of international telecommunications.

4. Discuss the problems versus the potential benefits of global networks.

5. Discuss some of the important issues relevant to the integration of various technologies on a global scale.

6. Discuss international applications such as Electronic Data Interchange (EDI) that are made possible by advancements in international telecommunications.

SUGGESTED READINGS

Banberg, R. A. "Global Networking." *Telecommunications* (December 1990): 57–59.

Keen, Peter G. W. *Competing in Time: Using Telecommunications for Competitive Advantage.* Massachusetts: Ballinger, 1988.

Langford, G. "Planning the Multinational Network." *Telecommunications* (November 1989): 27–28.

Muroyama, Janet H. and H. Guyford Stever, eds. *Globalization of Technology: International Perspectives.* Washington, D.C.: National Academy Press, 1988.

Runyan, Linda. "Global IS Strategies." *Datamation* (December 1, 1989): 71–78.

Salso, E. L. "How PTTs are Going Multinational." *Long Range Planning* (February 1990): 136–146.

Solomon, A. H. "Telecommunications in the 1990s—Managing Networks to Serve User Needs." *Telecommunications* (February 1990): 23–27.

Chapter S I X

STRATEGIC PLANNING FOR INTERNATIONAL INFORMATION SYSTEMS

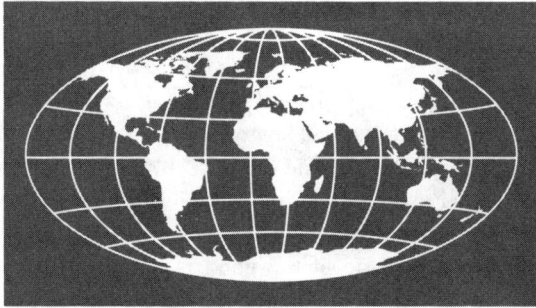

The need for Information Systems (IS) planning is not a new phenomenon. Strategic planning for a firm's information resources continues to be ranked in numerous studies as one of the top priorities among MIS executives.[1] In today's business environment strategic planning cannot occur only domestically. As the globalization of industries and markets continues its rapid evolution, the impact of changing business conditions and increased competition on a firm in one country will have a simultaneous impact on the firm's operations in other countries. The strategic planning process adopted by the firm must reflect this dual impact.

In this chapter, we will discuss four areas related to the strategic

IS planning process. First, we will focus our attention on the environmental factors driving the need for strategic international information systems planning. Second, we will develop an understanding of the firm's changing information system requirements as its operations evolve from a purely domestic to a global orientation. Third, we will present an approach for assessing the current status of a firm's international information systems and we will identify the barriers to the creation of an international IS plan. Fourth, we will compare the key attributes of strategic IS planning in the domestic and international environments and present a strategic planning framework for the development of an international IS plan.

THE NEED FOR GLOBAL INFORMATION SYSTEMS PLANNING

There are two primary forces driving the need for global IS planning: increased trade and foreign direct investment, and the accelerating advancement of information technology.

Over the past two decades the business environment has been undergoing a dramatic shift. Since 1970 the growth in the volume of international trade has surpassed the growth of total world gross national product (GNP). Today, the volume of world trade is seven times larger than total world GNP.[2] This means that the value added activities associated with international business are spread across many countries with the result that the value of the good is substantially greater than the sum of its raw materials and components.

At the same time, the advancement of information technology has proceeded at an unprecedented rate. For example, the basic research needed to develop the transistor at Bell Laboratories in 1947 took more than a decade and it was another ten years before the transistor was incorporated into the computer and successfully marketed. In contrast, it took only three years for the integrated circuit developed by Texas Instruments in 1958 to reach the marketplace, thus substantially increasing the price-performance ratios of computer hardware by a factor of ten. Today, technological change occurs within months, as evidenced by the rapid evolution from 16-kilobyte to 1-megabyte microchips.

Together, the globalization of business and the rapid advancements of information technology drive economic changes and raise uncertainty levels, leading to higher business risk. With increased risk, there follows a need for strategic planning of the firm's information resources in the global environment.

Advancement of Information Technology

Information technology enables managers to perform a variety of tasks that were once done by subordinates. For example, in our daily routine most of us use a personal computer and word processing software to write letters, prepare reports, and create presentations. Just fifteen years ago, we wrote letters longhand on a pad of paper and had a secretary type them. Information technology has enabled us to do more work in less time and has given us the capability to present more information in a variety of formats. In essence, it has completely changed the way we work.

Investing in information technology gives firms a competitive advantage in the marketplace through increased coordination and control of its activities. For example, point-of-sale terminals not only provide a means of collecting money and recording transactions but also provide top managers with minute-to-minute information about sales levels, product performance, shelf utilization, advertising effectiveness, and inventory levels. These terminals eliminate the need for restocking orders because orders are automatically sent at predetermined reorder points to vendors through electronic date interchange (EDI) facilities. At General Electric's Appliance Park in Louisville, Kentucky, information technology has eliminated the need for the material requirements department to issue individual purchase orders to overseas suppliers. When a manufacturing facility needs additional parts, the order is automatically placed with the vendor through an EDI system. The role of purchasing at GE has changed from a primarily accounting-oriented function to that of a worldwide sourcing and vendor qualification function.

The advancement of information technology on a global scale has given rise to a new definition for information system applications that cross national borders. A global information technology application is one that contributes to the firm's global business strategy by using information technology platforms to manipulate data across cultural environments.[3] For example, banks have developed information technology applications that enable their customers to obtain local currency from their home-country checking accounts while traveling in any other country. The system enables the bank to identify the customer, convert the home currency to local currency at current market exchange rates, and instantaneously debit that person's account.

Global information technology applications collapse time and distance to enable corporations to conduct business twenty-four hours a day while almost completely eliminating information float—the time between the creation of the information and its use. Some large computer firms use a team of product development specialists located in Europe, the United States, and Japan to develop new software products. Information technology allows product development to take place twenty-four hours a day, eliminating the need for all members of the product development team to be in the same physical location.

IBM, for example, uses a research team in Hursley, England; San Jose, California; and Tokyo, Japan to develop some of their new commercial software systems. When the team in England is finished for the day, the product database is transferred via telecommunications facilities to California where the San Jose team is just arriving for work. When the California team is done for the day, the product then moves to Japan and onward again to England. Global information technology substantially reduces the development time required to get a product to market and saves the cost of travel for researchers located around the world. This means that a company can team its best people together from anywhere in the world to develop and market a product in less time at less cost. This use of information technology results in a competitive advantage for the firm.

Historically, the development and application of new information technology was the domain of companies located in developed countries, specifically, the United States. Information systems in the United States were first developed because of easy access to the latest technology, knowledgeable users, and in-house data processing expertise. Initially, U.S. companies were only able to take advantage of information technology in their domestic operations. However, as other nations developed their information technology infrastructures and as the number of non-U.S. computer vendors grew, the U.S. multinational corporation began to apply information technology in its overseas subsidiaries. The use of automated payroll and accounting systems were the first applications to be transferred abroad. These were quickly followed by manufacturing and marketing information systems.

Often automated, these systems were primarily stand-alone applications. For example, the payroll system used in a French subsidiary may have been developed separately from the system used in Japan. Through the development of telecommunications, information technology has advanced to the point where these systems are interconnected among operating subsidiaries. Today, subsidiaries are accessing the same databases in real-time environments or exchanging information needed to manage a fragmented production process by tying together the ordering procedures of several plants with suppliers located on other continents.

The rapid advancement of information technology has necessitated the use of strategic planning as a management tool for dealing with the complexity created by the new technology. Without careful strategic planning, management cannot take advantage of the new technologies and applications that are being developed on a daily basis. Strategic planning enables the firm to smooth the transition from one technology to the next. In an environment where the time span between technology development and its application is reduced from years to months, strategic planning is the only tool available that provides management maximum benefit from its investment in information technology.

By itself, information technology has a profound impact on the way business is conducted around the world. Consequently, there is a need to establish more formal and comprehensive strategic planning approaches. The international application of this technology to business problems creates higher levels of complexity for managers trying to coordinate and control the activities of a firm that operates twenty-four hours a day in many markets around the world.

Globalization of Industries

We have briefly discussed the impact of advanced information technology on the firm. We will now discuss the pattern of competition that varies from industry to industry. For example, the industry structure and operating characteristics of the medical instruments industry are very different from those of the sporting goods industry. Industry patterns also vary according to the degree of internationalization. Globalization or internationalization can be visualized along a spectrum of competition.

On one end of the spectrum are multidomestic industries in which competition from country to country is essentially independent. This means that an industry may exist in many countries (for example, retail banking in the United States, France, or Canada) but competition within each country is independent and not affected by that in other countries. Firms competing in multidomestic industries gain a competitive advantage from their successful activities in an individual country. The firm may derive a one-time advantage by transferring technological know-how from the home country, but the technology must be adapted to meet the specific needs of that country. Since the firm competes on a country-by-country basis, such adaptations have little impact on the operations of multidomestic firms.

The implication for strategic planning in multidomestic industries is that business unit planning can be done independently by country. In terms of information technology applications, a parent organization can transfer applications developed in one country to another country, but they must be completely adapted to the second country's environment—essentially becoming new applications. Strategic planning for information systems in a multidomestic environment can be conducted on a country-by-country basis with little or no consideration of the impact of these systems from one country to another.

On the other end of the competitive spectrum are global industries. There is a profound difference between the operation of firms competing in global industries and in multidomestic industries. The global industry is not merely a collection of individual country markets and operations but a series of linked domestic industries in which rivals compete against each other on a truly worldwide basis.[4] Examples of global industries include television, automobile, and semiconductor manufacturers. In global industries the firm must manage its activities on an integrated basis if it is to achieve an advantage over its competitors. The implications for international information systems planning in this environment are considerable. In contrast to a multidomestic industry in which the firm operates on a country-centered basis with high degrees of autonomy among its data processing operations, the global firm must seek to coordinate and integrate its information systems across all countries in which it operates. The dual imperative involves balancing the degree of adaptation given to information system applications in one country with the need to standardize and share systems across many countries.

The globalization of industries and markets demands that multinational corporations make the transition from a portfolio of country-centered business strategies to an integrated global strategy based on achieving a high level of coordination and integration among the firm's activities on a worldwide basis. Strategic planning in this environment is essential for firms trying to manage business operations that have a high degree of complexity. If the purpose of strategic information systems planning is to link the information systems resources of the firm to the business plan and to assist the firm in achieving its overall business objectives, planning for international information systems must also reflect a high degree of coordination and integration across national borders.

THE EVOLUTION OF INTERNATIONAL INFORMATION SYSTEMS PLANNING

Rarely does a company become a multinational corporation as the result of a single decision by top management to "go" international. The process of becoming a multinational organization is best viewed as an evolutionary process in which management continuously develops higher levels of international business activity and a global orientation. Most firms evolve through distinctive incremental stages in which they gain international experience, broaden their business activities, and develop an organizational structure and philosophy that transcend the borders of any one nation. Figure 6–1 illustrates the key business operations characteristics of the firm as it evolves into a global enterprise.

The figure shows five stages in the evolution of a multinational enterprise. These include exporting, direct sales, direct production, full autonomy, and global integration. Within each stage there are strategic variables that mark the evolution of internationalization of the firm. These descriptive variables, called *strategic characteristics,* are divided into two categories: business operations and information systems. The business operations include the orientation or strategic view of management, the organization structure, the strategic mode of management, the mode of market entry, and the approach to business planning. Accompanying the firm's characteristics within each stage of the evolutionary process are four information system elements that characterize the evolution of a firm's international information resources. These include the application portfolio, technical resources, management techniques, and the end user.

To better understand the strategic planning process for international information systems, we need to examine the dynamics of the firm's information technology evolution within the context of the internationalization of the enterprise. The following discussion describes the evolution of the enterprise and its information system at each stage of the evolutionary process.

Stage I: Exporting

Many corporations enter foreign markets as the result of receiving an unsolicited order from overseas. These orders are handled like any domestic order except that the firm must comply with various legal and financial requirements. Some of these requirements include applying for

Strategic Characteristics	Stage I *Exporting*	Stage II *Direct Sales*	Stage III *Direct Production*	Stage IV *Full Autonomy*	Stage V *Global Integration*
Business Operations Characteristics					
Firm orientation	Ethnocentric	Ethnocentric	Polycentric	Polycentric	Geocentric
Organizational structure	Export department	International division	Product division	Geographic area	Product/area matrix
Planning approach	Ad hoc	Country-centered	Product-based	Portfolio	Dual structure
Strategic mode	Entreprenuerial	Entreprenuerial	Adaptive	Adaptive	Integrative
Market entry	Agents/distributors	Foreign sales office	Joint venture	Wholly-owned subsidiaries	Multiple subsidiaries and joint ventures

Information Systems Characteristics					
Application portfolio	Shipping, customs, and credit documents	Accounting, payroll, and office systems	Accounting, office, and manufacturing	Full portfolio of applications	Common applications and data bases
Technical resources	PC-based network	Stand-alone, PC-based	Stand-alone mainframe and PC-network	Multiple stand-alone and PC-based systems	Regional DP centers and networked systems
Management techniques	Domestic MIS support	Local support	Technology transfer, local support staff	Local and regional support staffs	Multi-level. Corporate, regional and local
Users	Few. Sales, shipping, and accounting dept.	Few. Local and domestic users	Many. Local users	Many. Local and regional users	Many users worldwide

FIGURE 6–1 Evolution of the Multinational Enterprise—Strategic Business Operations and Information Systems Characteristics

an export license, obtaining letters of credit, and arranging for freight forwarders and insurance carriers. At first, one person may be responsible for handling the specialized documentation, but as the volume of orders increases the firm may establish an export department within the domestic sales and marketing function.

The firm's orientation toward international markets can be described as ethnocentric. The focus of senior management and the orientation of the firm's marketing and manufacturing activities are dominated by the domestic market. Traditionally, most U.S. firms are ethnocentric because of the large size and sufficiency of the domestic market. Given the firm's domestic orientation and organizational structure, there is no formal business planning for foreign markets. If international planning is done, it is usually of an ad hoc nature (performed by the manager responsible for the export department). The export manager usually takes an entrepreneurial approach and aggressively seeks agents and distributors to sell the firm's product abroad. However, at this stage of development, the firm has little or no control over how the product is marketed, priced, or serviced after the sale.

Typically, firms in Stage I are exporters with varying degrees of activity. The firms usually have not developed any specialized information systems applications. The export department may be using spreadsheets to determine pricing levels, foreign exchange exposure, and hedging alternatives but with little or no assistance by the MIS group. Most of the information is stored manually and transmitted via facsimile and telex equipment to agents and distributors abroad. Because overseas agents and distributors are separate enterprises, there is no need for the MIS department to support their computing requirements. Essentially, there is no international information system in Stage-I firms and consequently the need for strategic planning is nonexistent.

Stage II: Direct Sales

The typical evolution of a firm in the international marketplace is evidenced by an increasing percentage of the firm's total sales coming from overseas markets. It is not unusual for firms to experience higher growth rates for their products in overseas markets than in the domestic market. This is particularly true as the product enters the maturity stage of the product life cycle. Often, when the growth in overseas markets exceeds growth in the domestic market, senior management becomes much more interested in international business.

Although the firm still has an ethnocentric orientation, management seeks to have more control over the marketing of its products abroad. Having gained valuable experience in working with overseas agents and distributors, the firm may now open its own foreign sales and marketing office. The firm undertakes this move for several reasons. First, the profit margins are much higher without using an agent, and second, the firm can gain valuable market exposure and experience if its own employees are located in the foreign market. As the growing volume of overseas sales becomes sufficient, the firm may adopt an international division structure. At this point, the firm will give focused management attention to the foreign market, dictating the need for strategic business planning.

Strategic business planning for these markets is now performed by the international division managers on a country-by-country basis with each operation being treated separately from the others. The strategic approach of the firm in Stage II remains entrepreneurial, allowing it to operate outside of the corporate planning structure.

The international division is supported by its own marketing, finance, and accounting staff. However, information systems support still remains in other organizational units reporting to a vice president for information resources or within a functional division to a vice president for finance and administration. In the headquarters location, the international applications portfolio of the international division includes the automation of shipping, customs, and accounting documents required by the international staff. Most of these applications are PC-based with few applications being run on the firm's mainframe system. Similar to other divisions of the company, the international division is connected to the corporate information system for applications such as electronic mail, inventory status, and other accounting systems.

While the international division headquarters is part of the corporate information system, the same is usually not true of the foreign sales operations. When first established, the overseas branch offices are not part of the corporate network. In general, they function as stand-alone systems because the office employs a small staff. In this case, the office utilizes a PC-based system for office, payroll, and general accounting applications.

Planning for international information systems in this stage of the evolution is performed by the local branch office staff with advice from the international division staff. Plans focus primarily on standardizing branch office procedures and may include the development of a branch office network using a third-party, value added network such as General Electric's Information System (GEIS). The development of this network occurs only when the number and size of branch offices become fairly large and the volume of overseas sales is substantial. This generally occurs towards the end of Stage II.

Stage III: Direct Production

The development of overseas production capability is a significant strategic decision for the firm. This is done to take advantage of lower cost production and to access markets not available to the firm through direct export. At this stage of the evolution, the firm's orientation can be described as polycentric. Senior management thinks of its business in terms of multiple countries or regions, each being an integral part of the firm though the domestic market is still considered the most important.

The establishment of overseas production facilities may coincide with a reorganization of the firm into a product division structure. In this structure each product division is responsible for the manufacturing and marketing of its products worldwide. For example, Procter & Gamble is organized on a product division basis. The hair care products division is responsible for the production and marketing of the firm's shampoos, conditioners, and other hair-related products worldwide.

The business planning shifts from a country-specific approach to a product-based approach. This means that the firm is trying to rationalize its production so that it can produce fairly standardized products at the lowest cost for distribution worldwide. This requires a high level of coordination among the various manufacturing locations and suppliers. The strategic mode of operation is adaptive in the sense that the firm is trying to respond to overseas competition by producing a standardized product at the lowest price for consumers in many markets.

In Stage III of the firm's multinational evolution, the information systems characteristics are also changing and have an impact on the strategic planning process. As manufacturing facilities are built, they require cost-accounting systems, materials requirements planning systems, and other computer-based information systems. In the early phases of Stage III, these systems are implemented through technology transfer programs from the domestic operation. The information systems are adapted to fit into each plant environment and function as stand-alone systems using a combination of mini-, mainframe-, and PC-based equipment and software.

Support for these manufacturing systems is provided by the local staff with consulting support from the domestic MIS group.

Strategic planning for international information systems is accomplished separately from domestic planning and is usually plant or country specific. Toward the end of Stage III, there may be a need for the various manufacturing sites to communicate electronically with each other, and to some extent the strategic plan must provide for coordination of worldwide manufacturing.

Stage IV: Full Autonomy

In this stage of the evolution, corporations have attained a size and scope in their international operations such that they are considered truly worldwide. The firm not only produces and sells in many countries but also conducts research and development and many support functions, such as finance and personnel, abroad on a regional basis.

The multinational corporation at this stage is usually organized on a geographic basis to focus its managerial skill and resources on specific country markets. For example, when IBM was in Stage IV, the company consisted of many wholly-owned subsidiaries that functioned autonomously from the U.S. operations. IBM-Japan and IBM-France each functioned as separate companies, each possessing its own research, manufacturing, and marketing functions somewhat independent of one another. Their primary impetus was to respond to the needs of the country-markets where they were headquartered.

The information systems for Stage IV firms consist of many fully autonomous data centers reporting to each subsidiary headquarters. Each subsidiary is supported through its own local and regional technical resources. Planning for these information systems is the responsibility of each subsidiary. The role of the parent organization and its MIS headquarters group primarily involves consulting and coordination of activities. Strategic planning for international information systems is conducted by each subsidiary with the headquarters staff providing information from the other subsidiaries and establishing the guidelines and standards to be followed in the planning process.

Stage V: Global Integration

Very few corporations in the world have reached Stage V in their evolution. Only the largest firms in the world such as General Motors, IBM, Toyota, Siemens, and Mitsubishi, with fully developed operations and organizational structures around the world, fall into the Stage-V category. A characteristic of these firms is their geocentric orientation. These firms do not view any one country as being more important to the firm than any other country. The orientation of the firm is singularly global. Products developed in one country are simultaneously marketed around the world.

Firms that have evolved to this stage are faced with the challenge of being responsive to national markets while still rationalizing their activities on a global scale to achieve competitive advantage from standardization. This is referred to as the *dual imperative*. Corporations attempt to balance the demands of the dual imperative through organizational structures called *matrix organizations*. Firms with matrix structures are organized on both a geographic and a product basis. The matrix forces product managers that have worldwide development and manufacturing responsibilities to coordinate and work with country or regional managers who have geographic responsibilities. The product manager's goal is to produce products of a standardized nature that achieve low-cost objectives, while the geographic managers want to sell products that are adapted to the specific requirements and tastes of individual country markets.

The dual structure reflects a strategic mode of the firm to be integrative in its operations. The planning approach also reflects this orientation to coordinate and integrate the firm's operations on a global basis. The implications of this orientation and structure for strategic international information systems are enormous.

The information systems of the firm can be characterized as a multiplicity of data centers, applications, users, and vendors representing many nationalities. At this stage of development a large investment has been made in the firm's information systems infrastructure around the world. The challenge is to create a strategic international information systems plan that links these systems to the business environment in which the firm is trying to integrate its operations on a worldwide basis.

In this planning environment, the parent headquarters group responsible for MIS takes on a new planning role. The role is complex because the group must balance the need to establish standards, guidelines, common applications, and data bases that achieve fully integrated international systems, with the needs of each country affiliate that is trying to develop local systems responsive to the needs of local management. This is a task that is increasingly complex and that places the role of strategic planning as a high priority.

In the discussion that follows, we will examine how multinational corporations undertake strategic planning for international systems. We will examine the strategic planning process by contrasting international and domestic attributes, and we will identify the barriers to the creation of an international plan. Finally, we will discuss a typical planning approach and present a general framework for the development of a strategic international information systems planning process.

ASSESSING THE STATUS OF INTERNATIONAL IS

For many firms, the growth of international information systems is not the result of years of strategic planning and implementation. Instead, the systems develop on an ad hoc basis as business requirements dictate. As we have discussed, the nature of the firm's international information systems is largely dependent on the current stage of evolution in the multinational corporation's operations. For some firms, this means that each subsidiary establishes its own information systems independently of the parent organization. In others, the international information systems are simply an extension of the domestic operation. Senior management's recognition of the importance of its international operations and the need for strategic planning usually result in an assessment of the current status in international information processing before adopting a strategic planning process.

Assessing the current status of the firm's international information processing operations makes the system more responsive to the needs of the business. As a one-time endeavor, this assessment will provide a plan for the future. To use an analogy, it is similar to renovating a house to meet the future needs of the owners. An architect must first have accurate plans of the existing foundation; structural, electrical, and plumbing systems; and room layouts before drafting plans to improve the function of the entire home. The same is true for international systems.

To assess the current status of operations, senior management needs to focus on four key areas.[5] These include: (1) an examination of the nature of the information flows to management, (2) a comprehensive understanding of current long-range business and information systems planning practices, (3) an understanding of the responsibilities and structure of the international data processing operation, and (4) an assessment of the cost of information processing by region and business unit. A questionnaire such as the one shown in Figure 6–2 can be used to make an initial assessment of the firm's international data processing operation.

According to Martin Buss, the questionnaire's author, senior management needs to take action in three ways. First, it is recommended that senior management actively orchestrate the process by which the organization approaches its planning for international data processing. Second, an organizational framework for strategic planning of international information systems should be created. Third, senior management needs to identify and define the role of the key players in the process.

Task Force on International Computing

In large organizations that have worldwide operations and many subsidiaries, a task force on international data processing is often established by the senior management of the company. The task force makes

	Nature of the Information Provided	Yes	No
1.	Can I compare operating results across affiliates in a way that helps me form conclusions on relative product costs, margins, and sales volumes?	☐	☐
2.	Do I know whether my subordinates are satisfied with their information resources?	☐	☐
3.	Do I know whether my competitors have better information systems than I do?	☐	☐
	Business and Data Processing		
4.	Have I approved a long-range information systems plan?	☐	☐
5.	Do I know whether the data-processing plan supports my business plans for the key regions?	☐	☐
6.	Has data processing been on the agenda of high-level operations reviews in the past 6 months?	☐	☐
7.	In the past 12 months have I been involved in any major decisions on an information-processing issue?	☐	☐
8.	Have I been briefed in the past 12 months on the implications of new information-processing technology for my business?	☐	☐

Organization of Data Processing

9. Do I know how international data-processing
   responsibilities are organized?   ☐ ☐

10. Do I have the authority and responsibility to get
    the information processing I want?   ☐ ☐

11. Do I have a source that keeps me informed as to
    how well data processing is working?   ☐ ☐

Cost of Information Processing

12. Do I know how much I am spending on data
    processing in my key regions?   ☐ ☐

13. Do I know whether these regions are spending
    enough, too much, or too little?   ☐ ☐

14. Do I know on which functions data-processing
    emphasis is being placed for the current levels of
    expenditure?   ☐ ☐

15. Do I think this emphasis is in the right place?   ☐ ☐

Total

(Yes)
SCORE: *12 or more* indicates that information processing
operations are saved and well coordinated.

6–11 suggests management intervention in some
areas is needed.

Below 6 serious problems.

FIGURE 6-2   Rating the International DP Operation

Source: Copyright © 1982 by the President and Fellows of Harvard College. All
rights reserved. Reprinted by permission of *Harvard Business Review,* "Managing International Information Systems," by Martin D. J. Buss, September–October 1982,
vol. 60, p. 158.

recommendations about the approach the firm should use to establish a
strategic planning framework and implementation procedure. Often, the
team or task force includes a wide mix of individuals representing data-
processing and nondata-processing areas of the business. In some task
force groups the mix would include managers from a variety of product
divisions, host countries, and functional areas. As a working guideline,
the task force may divide its activities into the four areas of the questionnaire in Figure 6–2. While these are important starting points, the
task force also needs to consider broader issues that may have an impact

on the approach recommended to senior management. Some of these broader issues may include:[6]

- the nature of the business in each country and the role of information systems in attaining the corporation's long-term goals
- the structure of the organization and role of staff versus line management in each subsidiary operation; the power in decision making between headquarters staff and country line management
- the cultural characteristics and personalities of the individuals responsible for the firm's international business and data processing operations
- the history of each country's organization and involvement in data processing
- the impact of host-country government regulations on the business and its accompanying data-processing operations
- the extent to which technology transfer takes place between the parent organization and its subsidiaries, and among the country's subsidiaries themselves

Creating the Framework

The assessment by the firm's task force on international information systems should include recommendations on the strategic framework or approach to be used by the firm to plan and organize the international data-processing operations. These recommendations should address the following issues:[7]

- an organizational structure for international data processing
- establishment of responsibility for standards relating to hardware and software systems
- location and ownership of the firm's data centers abroad
- determination of which data centers country managers would use, either in the host country or regional data centers
- identification of the resources for technical support of each subsidiary operation
- establishment of an international steering committee or international computer council, including membership and areas of oversight

Defining the Roles of Key Players

The task force on international computing must define the roles of key individuals if the work of the task force is to be implemented in a manner consistent with the information requirements of the business. The strategic planning process that the firm ultimately adopts and uses is dependent on clearly defining these roles. At least the four following areas need to be addressed by the task force defining the key roles of management.

Top management, specifically the senior executive responsible for the firm's international business operations, must clearly state the objectives of the business strategy so that the international computer council or steering committee can translate these business objectives into information systems objectives.

A policy for implementation must be established before any strategic planning process so that country managers and headquarters staff understand who has ultimate responsibility for implementing the projects needed to attain the firm's stated information systems goals.

The international computer council needs to be provided with an on-going supply of information and a vehicle for coordinating the data processing-related activities of each subsidiary. Identification of international information coordinators to serve this function should also be an end product of the work of this task force.

A high degree of cooperation is required between country subsidiaries and data processing and business unit management. To ensure that the potential of international information processing is fully realized, line management in each country must be identified and given the responsibility for contributing to the implementation and management of the firm's international computing activities.

Many companies invest a large amount of time and money in assessing the status of their firm's current international data processing. These multinational corporations undertake task-force studies, create international computer councils, and carefully define the roles of key individuals. But in spite of these efforts, there are many barriers to the creation of an effective international information systems plan.

BARRIERS TO CREATING AN INTERNATIONAL IS PLAN

After assessing the need to restructure a firm's international data processing operations, senior executives are often confronted with internal and external barriers to the creation of a strategic international IS plan.[8] The barriers to the development and implementation of a strategic plan are illustrated in Figure 6–3. The external barriers include regulatory differences and international standards imposed by the environment in which the firm operates. The internal barriers that confront senior management include managerial knowledge, diffusion of organizational authority, and cultural/language differences.

External Barriers

Management must understand the limitations that external barriers place on the development of an effective strategic plan and must seek ways to neutralize their impact on the implementation of the firm's strategic information systems. In contrast, the internal barriers include issues of managerial awareness and education. We will begin with an examination of the external barriers to a strategic international IS plan followed by a discussion of the internal barriers.

Regulatory differences among host country governments vary widely. As we discussed in our examination of transborder data flows (Chapter 4), public monopolies such a PTT are used by many host country governments to constrain competition and achieve certain national economic goals. Because most PTTs are revenue-oriented rather than access-

---

External

- Regulatory differences
- International standards

Internal

- Managerial knowledge
- Diffusion of organizational authority
- Cultural/language differences

FIGURE 6–3   Barriers to the Development and Implementation of a Strategic International Information Systems Plan

oriented, the foreign firm is usually prevented from taking advantage of telecommunications economies of scale and innovations in their computing technology.

Because the PTT is the only provider of telecommunications facilities in many countries, there is no impetus for the implementation of new technologies in areas such as fiber optics, switching equipment, and satellites. As a result, the multinational corporation is often faced with the task of trying to patch together a telecommunications network among the countries in which the firm operates.

Continuously changing regulations have an impact on the telecommunications elements of the firm's international information systems operations in other countries. The regulatory barrier is created in many cases because the foreign firm does not understand or participate in the process of developing new regulations. For example, a large U.S. money center bank made a strategic decision to expand its branch operations in a South American country. The strategic business plan called for the implementation of an advanced ATM teller network to cover many urban and rural areas of the country. Because the IS department lacked an understanding of future telecommunications regulation in that country, a strategic IS plan could not be implemented to support the business plan.

International standards create another external barrier for firms trying to develop a strategic international information systems plan. In many countries, standards determine the computing options available to the firm. They range from details about connecting hardware to procedures and protocols involving database management and telecommunications software.

In the international environment, there are three forums through which standards become established: committees, vendors, and customers. It often takes years for these standards to be established and, even then, there are many deviations from country to country. International standards established through quasi-governmental committees attempt to provide long-term models that firms can incorporate into their planning. As discussed earlier, an example is the Open Systems Interconnect (OSI) standard for all communications and computer hardware interconnections. In contrast, vendor supplied systems such as IBM's Systems Network Architecture (SNA) become de facto standards because of the market power of a vendor corporation. However, this may lock a firm into hardware or software decisions that are incompatible in some countries in which the firm operates. In the third forum, the standard is dictated by a firm's customer. For example, General Motor's Manufacturing Automotive Protocol (MAP) must be adopted by any company wishing to do business with GM.

The establishment of standards around the world facilitates the formulation and implementation of a strategic IS Plan. Understanding these standards and their variations within countries is essential to the development of information systems that support the business operation around the world.

Internal Barriers

There are also internal barriers to developing a strategic international information systems plan. Perhaps the most important barrier is also the most difficult to change—managerial knowledge. The senior managers and technical staff responsible for an organization's information systems have little or no international experience. Traditionally, the information needs of the headquarters were simply sent to the local manager, usually a foreign national, without much involvement from the management information systems staff. The need to develop global business strategies that coordinate and integrate a firm's activities in many countries now requires that senior managers responsible for developing the international IS plan have first-hand experience with the IS environment of the firm's host country operations. Without this experience and knowledge, the quality of the strategic IS plan and its ability to support the global business plan are very low. The fact that equipment and hardware may be standardized from region to region does not mean that procedures, tasks, and management decisions needed to implement the IS plan are also standardized.

A second internal barrier to the creation and implementation of a strategic IS plan is the diffusion of organizational authority. As senior executives in multinational enterprises continue to decentralize decision making in order to be more responsive to local market and country conditions, there is an even greater need for central coordination. With business unit authority for decisions residing at the regional or country level, managers can override headquarter's mandates for standardization if local business conditions warrant. As a result, it is very difficult for a headquarter's technical group to implement a telecommunications plan and other large, company-wide projects. For example, a manager for a U.S. bank subsidiary in Taiwan grew impatient waiting for an international cash management program that was to be standardized around the world using IBM equipment and custom software. He chose instead to purchase a WANG-based system using third-party software and had the system operating in only a few months. From the perspective of the local business managers, it was a sound decision. However, from the perspective of corporate IS managers who are concerned about standardization, it was not a good decision. The managerial challenge is to balance centralized coordination with decentralized decision making.

A third internal barrier to the development and implementation of strategic information systems is the diversity of languages and cultures within the multinational corporate organization. A large organization may operate in as many as 120 countries—each with its own unique language, customs, and business practices. Even though the company's official business language is English, each subsidiary must translate the information systems plan into the vocabulary and terms of the local data processing staff responsible for the plan's implementation. Ensuring that the same results are consistent across borders becomes a very difficult task.

ATTRIBUTES OF STRATEGIC *IS* PLANNING—DOMESTIC VERSUS INTERNATIONAL

The similarities and differences between strategic planning in the domestic and international environments can best be understood by comparing the attributes of the various components of the planning framework. The planning elements include environment, planning process, business philosophy and style, planning responsibilities, plan posture, technology, and plan monitoring and control.[9] The domestic and international attributes of the seven planning elements are summarized in Figure 6–4 and discussed below.

Environment

The environment in which strategic planning for information systems takes place varies according to language, cultural, legal, political, and geographic attributes. Essentially, the planning process in the domestic and international environments differs in terms of the number of environments that must be considered. In the domestic environment, where a single culture and set of political and legal issues affect the firm, planning is somewhat easier. Internationally, a multiplicity of environments that interact with each other must be considered, compounding the complexity of the planning task. Therefore, a firm operating in several

FIGURE 6-4 Comparison of Domestic and International Information Resource Management (IRM) Planning Attributes

Planning Elements	Domestic Attributes	International Attributes (Multiple Political Entities as Viewed from the Home Base)
1. Environment	Single language, nationality, and culture	Multilingual, multicultural, many nationalities
	One government and one body of regulations	Multigovernments and multiregulations
	Predominance of domestic vendors	National versus composite vendors
	Relatively homogeneous ISR resources and capabilities	Fragmented and diverse ISR resources and capabilities
	Relative level and degree of resource training and level of sophistication known	Fragmented resource training and degree and level of sophistication less known
	Relatively dependable level of ISR vendor support and relatively uniform coverage	Fragmented and unpredictable level of vendor support and nonuniform coverage
	Single geographic entity with limited time zone differences	Multiple geographic entities and multiple time zones
2. Planning Process: Environmental Analysis	Less complex with easier data collection	More complex with difficult and often inadequate data collection
Issue Assessment	Narrow and less complex	Multidimensional and more complex; more entities to consider
Number of Levels	Few—plants, divisions, corporate and functional groups	Many—plants, divisions, regions, countries, corporate and functional groups

Players	Information systems, telecommunications, office automation, users of one culture	Same, but for multiple cultures
Action Programs	Focus on domestic programs	Focus on domestic and international programs (e.g., technology migration, common systems, shared resources)
3. Business Philosophy and Style	Centralized, coordinated, or decentralized. Greater professional management disciplines	Ethnocentric, polycentric, or geocentric philosophy and information flows. Professional management disciplines vary by nationality as judged by U.S. criteria and not local criteria
4. MNISR Planning Responsibilities	Starting to be focused in one area (MIS) and more homogeneous	Fragmented, depending on country or region due to differences in local management philosophy and level of development
5. MNISR Plan Posture	More related to the business posture (passive or reactive versus proactive or opportunistic)	May be related to business posture but could be more strongly influenced by unions, tradition, and therefore, more difficult to accommodate than the domestic scene
6. Technology	Relatively sophisticated, known "State of the Art" technology available for every component of information systems resources	Wide variations in levels of available technology as well as usability. Due to lagging stages of development, technology is generally less sophisticated and sometimes, just not available (e.g., regulatory constraints) or transferabl *(continued)*

FIGURE 6–4, continued

7. Plan Monitoring and Control	Less difficult, fewer levels and audiences Easier to enforce standards and guidelines More common measurement criteria Relatively homogeneous strategies are more feasible (e.g., development, processing, realization of opportunities, planning, measurements)	More complex Degree and level of integration and information gathering more difficult to achieve National/regional goals may conflict with corporate and/or domestic goals and strategies Diverse forces are involved vis-à-vis the imposition of U.S. standards on foreign management, thus making the monitoring, control and coordination function very difficult

Source: Excerpt from *Strategic Planning for Information Resource Management: A Multinational Perspective,* copyright © 1983 by Gad Selig, is reprinted by permission of UMI Research Press, Ann Arbor, MI.

countries must consider not only each environment in which it operates but also interactions with the other country environments in which the firm plans its operation. For example, an American multinational corporation that has operations in France and Germany must understand not only the impact of each environment individually on its plans and operations but also the impact of possible interactions between the two environments (for example, trade policies, tariffs, export restrictions, work permits, vendor operations, and even time zones).

Planning Process

The strategic planning process for information systems consists of environmental analysis, issue assessment, number of planning levels, players, and action programs. In the domestic environment the analysis required in strategic planning is less complex, requiring data that are easier to collect than in the international environment. For example, assessing the environment in South America would require translations in both Spanish and Portuguese. In addition, the comparability of statistical information would often be limited because of differing methodologies used to collect the data. Data collected only in the United States for environmental analysis would not have this problem.

The number of divisions, plant locations, and branch offices adds to the complexity. Some multinational corporations operate as many as 5,000 offices around the world that must be incorporated into their planning process. Further compounding this complexity is the need to recognize that some users of information technology are more sophisticated than others. The educational background, skill levels, and stage of IS development often vary greatly from one country to another and must be considered carefully.

Business Philosophy and Style

The business philosophy of the company has an important impact on planning. In a purely domestic environment, the organization reflects one of three attitudes toward the firm's operations: centralized, decentralized, or coordinated. In an international context, the business philosophy reflects an ethnocentric, polycentric, or geocentric style. An ethnocentric firm sees its international operations through the eyes of its home country. Many companies see themselves as having an allegiance to their home country. A multinational corporation that views itself as an American company is ethnocentric in its philosophy. A polycentric firm sees itself as a collection of single-county business operations. A geocentric firm does not view its operations on a country basis and does not see itself as belonging to any one home country in the international environment. This style or business philosophy has a profound impact on the strategic planning process in addition to the issues of centralization, decentralization, and control found in the domestic setting.

Planning Responsibilities

In all centralized organizations and in most firms with decentralized structures, planning for the firm's information systems is the responsibility of a single group. The traditional domestic approach is to focus the responsibility for planning within the MIS department. However, in the international environment the responsibility for strategic planning is quite fragmented. In some areas it may be the responsibility of a regional headquarters, and in others, each country may be individually responsible. The reason for this fragmentation is due to the different managerial styles and level of organizational development that exist at the country-level operations of the firm.

Plan Posture

The posture of the strategic plan reflects the business orientation and may reflect a reactive or proactive approach to the marketplace and firm competition. In the domestic environment, the strategic IS plan primarily reflects the business plan posture. For example, an aggressive business plan that calls for the rapid expansion of branch offices in the United States would also have an accompanying strategic IS plan to provide the needed information network to support this rapid growth. However, in the international environment a proactive business plan does not necessarily result in a similar IS plan. Union restriction, government regulations, and other country-specific barriers may prevent an aggressive approach to the implementation of information systems that support the business plan.

Technology

In most developed countries corporations have access to sophisticated information technology. In the domestic environment the same technology can be applied across all geographical areas. For example, U.S.

banks can implement automated teller machine (ATM) technology in all fifty states. There is no difference between South Carolina and New York in terms of access or capability in applying ATM technologies. Unfortunately, this is not true in the international environment. Because of wide variations in the levels of availability and usability—due to lagging stages of information technology development or regulation from one country to another—a strategy that is easily applied in one country may not be feasible in another. In Indonesia, the lack of a reliable telecommunications infrastructure coupled with an unsophisticated information consumer prevent the widespread use of ATM machines. In the international environment, the strategic information systems plan must reflect the technology differences, whereas in the domestic environment, technology differences do not present such a problem.

Plan Monitoring and Control

An extremely important element of the strategic planning process is the capability to monitor and control the implementation of the plan. Again, the differences between the domestic and international environment are quite large. These differences are reflected in the number of management levels, enforcement of standards and guidelines, common measurement criteria, and diversity of the strategies being employed.

In the domestic environment, firm management of the monitoring and control process is less complex because fewer strategies are employed, measurement criteria are fairly standardized, and the number of units and levels of management tend to be small. In contrast, the complex international environment requires the firm to consider multiple measurement criteria, host government regulations that restrict company control, and the diversity of the firm's management from one country to another.

A STRATEGIC PLANNING FRAMEWORK

The process of strategic planning takes many forms and is normally tailored to the needs of the individual business. Figure 6–5 presents a basic strategic framework for planning a firm's international resources.[10] The framework is divided into six successive or integrated phases. In Phase 1, the strategic planning group answers the key question "Where are we today?" The answer to this question is based on an assessment of internal and external factors which leads the group to develop a strategic profile of its domestic and international information system

FIGURE 6-5   Theoretical Construct for Multinational Information Resource Management Strategic
Planning Phases

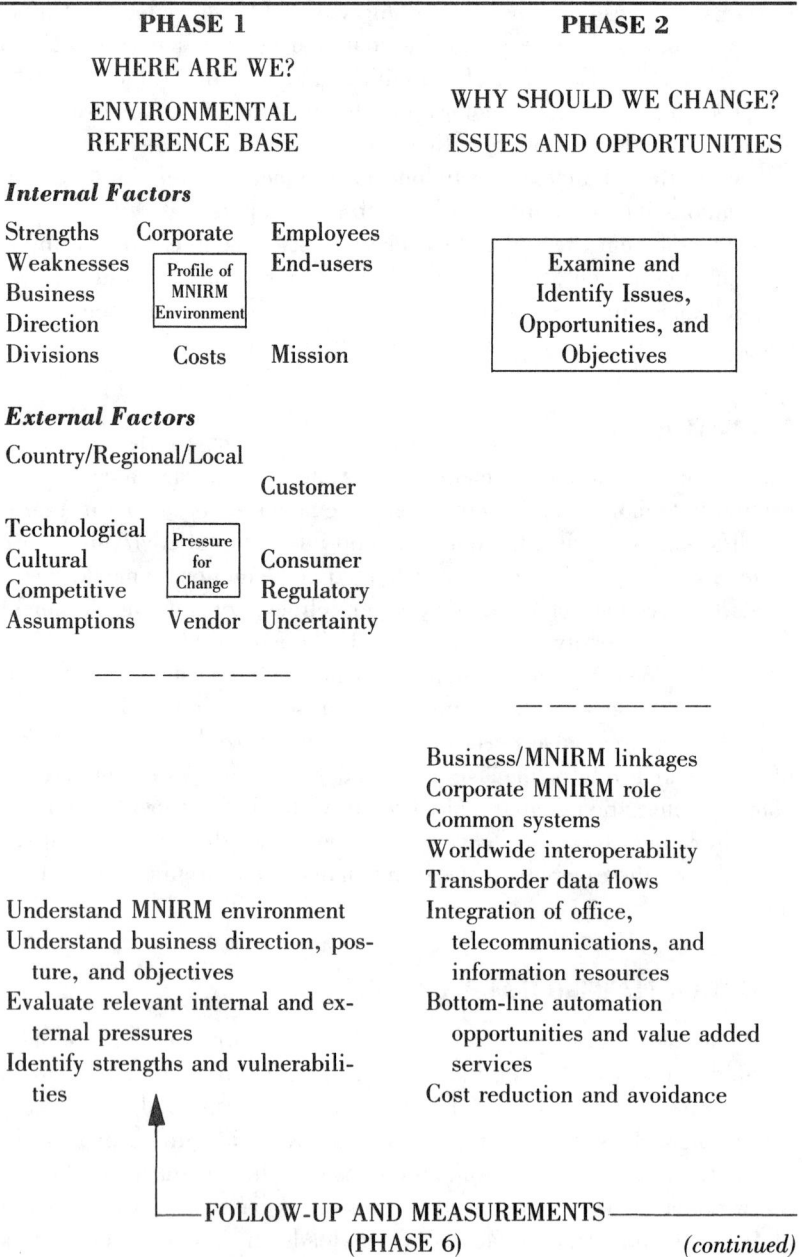

PHASE 1	PHASE 2
WHERE ARE WE?	
ENVIRONMENTAL REFERENCE BASE	WHY SHOULD WE CHANGE? ISSUES AND OPPORTUNITIES

Internal Factors

Strengths   Corporate   Employees
Weaknesses   [Profile of   End-users
Business   MNIRM
Direction   Environment]
Divisions   Costs   Mission

Examine and
Identify Issues,
Opportunities, and
Objectives

External Factors

Country/Regional/Local

                             Customer

Technological   [Pressure
Cultural   for   Consumer
Competitive   Change]   Regulatory
Assumptions   Vendor   Uncertainty

— — — — —

Understand MNIRM environment
Understand business direction, posture, and objectives
Evaluate relevant internal and external pressures
Identify strengths and vulnerabili-
  ties

— — — — —

Business/MNIRM linkages
Corporate MNIRM role
Common systems
Worldwide interoperability
Transborder data flows
Integration of office,
  telecommunications, and
  information resources
Bottom-line automation
  opportunities and value added
  services
Cost reduction and avoidance

└─FOLLOW-UP AND MEASUREMENTS─────
        (PHASE 6)   *(continued)*

FIGURE 6-5, continued

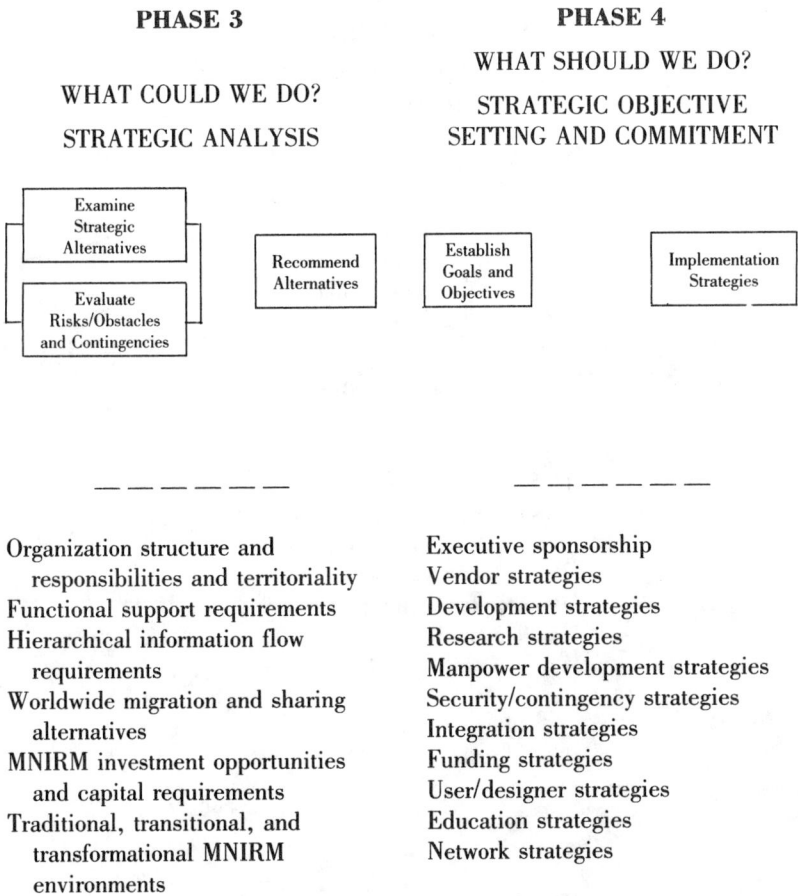

PHASE 3	PHASE 4
WHAT COULD WE DO?	WHAT SHOULD WE DO?
STRATEGIC ANALYSIS	STRATEGIC OBJECTIVE SETTING AND COMMITMENT

Examine Strategic Alternatives

Evaluate Risks/Obstacles and Contingencies

Recommend Alternatives

Establish Goals and Objectives

Implementation Strategies

Organization structure and
responsibilities and territoriality
Functional support requirements
Hierarchical information flow
requirements
Worldwide migration and sharing
alternatives
MNIRM investment opportunities
and capital requirements
Traditional, transitional, and
transformational MNIRM
environments

Executive sponsorship
Vendor strategies
Development strategies
Research strategies
Manpower development strategies
Security/contingency strategies
Integration strategies
Funding strategies
User/designer strategies
Education strategies
Network strategies

FOLLOW-UP AND MEASUREMENTS
(PHASE 6)   *(continued)*

FIGURE 6-5, continued

PHASE 5

HOW DO WE GET THERE?

SYSTEM DEVELOPMENT
METHODOLOGY

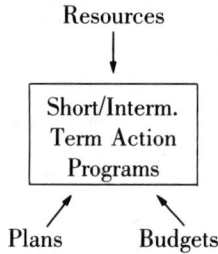

Resources

↓

```
┌─────────────────┐
│  Short/Interm.  │
│  Term Action    │
│  Programs       │
└─────────────────┘
```

↗   ↘

Plans   Budgets

— — — — — —

Resource allocation
System development methodology
Project approvals
Project plan monitoring
Implementation

———————————— FOLLOW-UP AND MEASUREMENTS ——→
(PHASE 6)

Source: Excerpt from: *Strategic Planning for Information Resource Management: A Multinational Perspective* copyright © 1983 by Gad Selig, is reprinted by permission of UMI Research Press, Ann Arbor, MI.

resources. A baseline or reference point is established by understanding the strengths and weaknesses of the current IS operation, the business direction of the firm, and the relevant internal and external pressures confronting the firm and its information resources.

As the strategic planning process enters its second phase, management must address the question "Why should we change?" Given the profile of the firm's current state of IS implementation, what are the key issues, opportunities, and objectives? In Phase 2, an examination of the linkages between the business plan and IS operation indicates changes needed to reallocate or realign the information systems strategy to better support the plan. This examination assesses key issues such as transborder data flows, the need for integrated support of specific elements of the business plan, and the role of the corporate IS staff in the process.

Based on conclusions from phases 1 and 2, the planning group should now understand the status of current IS resources and the obstacles, opportunities, and goals of the future IS operation. In Phase 3 of the planning process, management identifies possible strategic alternatives in terms of organization structure, information flows, migration to new systems, and other elements within the control of the IS function. The process requires that each alternative be evaluated and revised if necessary. A key component in the development of each alternative is a set of contingencies for each alternative plan.

A recommendation of the best strategy, based on advantages and disadvantages of alternative options, needs to be made to senior management. The Phase 4 question, "What should we do?" brings the planning process to a key decision point that involves the development of the actual plan including the required hardware, telecommunications, and software migration components. In addition, it identifies required personnel, training programs, and other nonequipment components of the plan.

The plan is further refined in Phase 5 through the development of a strategic road map that answers the question "How do we get there?" In this phase, the plan is translated into work areas and specific action plans. Important elements of these action plans are the resource requirements and budgets needed to implement each component of the plan.

Important to all strategic planning efforts is the need to measure the results, make adjustments, and follow up to ensure that the objectives of the plan are achieved. Phase 6 of the strategic planning process involves the use of a review mechanism based on preestablished milestones, measurable criteria, check points, standards, and guidelines to answer the question "Did we get there?"

SUMMARY

The strategic planning process for international information systems is complex because of the firm's multiple legal, political, social, and economic environments. The strategic international IS plan must support a business plan that addresses the pattern of competition faced by the firm, either multidomestic or global. As the firm evolves through the various stages of the internationalization process, the strategic international IS plan should address the various operating constraints and issues associated with each stage.

A basic approach to strategic planning for a firm's international information systems involves addressing the internal and external barriers and constraints in the international environment. The internal barriers include managerial knowledge limitations, the diffusion of authority within the organization, and the differences in language and culture among the firm's subsidiaries and headquarters. Two external barriers that must be addressed by the planning process are differences in host government laws and policies regulating business activity and constant problems associated with the lack of international standards.

It is also critical that management understand the differences in the key attributes of domestic versus international planning. One typology for understanding the complexity involved includes seven attributes: planning environment, planning process, business philosophy and style, planning responsibilities, plan posture, technology, and plan monitoring and control.

The strategic planning process adopted by an organization will vary from firm to firm. However, basic to most planning frameworks is a process that answers six key questions.

1. Where are we? (environmental reference phase)

2. Why should we change? (issues and opportunities)

3. What could we do? (strategic analysis)

4. What should we do? (strategic objective setting and commitment)

5. How do we get there? (systems development methodology)

6. Did we get there? (follow-up and measurement)

Strategic planning in the international environment is perhaps more critical than it is in the domestic environment because of the complexity that arises from addressing multiple political, legal, social, and economic systems. It is important to remember that strategic planning facilitates increased communication among the members of the organization worldwide who ultimately have responsibility for making the information system an effective resource for the enterprise.

NOTES

1. A. C. Boynton, and R. W. Zmud, "Information Technology Planning in the 1990s: Directions for Practice and Research," *MIS Quarterly* 11:1 (March 1987): 59–71.

2. United Nations Center on Transnational Corporations, *Salient Features and Trends in Foreign Direct Investment* (New York, NY: United Nations, 1984).

3. Blake Ives and Sirkka L. Jarvenpaa, "Applications of Global Information Technology: Key Issues for Management," *MIS Quarterly* (March 1991): 33–49.

4. Michael Porter, "Changing Patterns of International Competition," *California Management Review* (vol. XXVIII, no. 2, Winter 1986), 9–40.

5. Martin D. J. Buss, "Managing International Information Systems," *Harvard Business Review* (September–October 1982): 153–162.

6. G. J. Selig, *Strategic Planning for Information Resource Management: A Multinational Perspective* (Ann Arbor, Michigan: UMI Research Press, 1983). See also Suggested Readings by Buss, Ives and Jarvenpaa, and Selig.

7. Ibid.

8. Peter G. W. Keen, *An International Perspective on Managing Information Technologies* (Washington, DC: The International Center for Information Technology, 1987).

9. G. J. Selig, *Strategic Planning for Information Resource Management: A Multinational Perspective* (Ann Arbor, Michigan: UMI Research Press, 1983).

10. Ibid.

STUDY QUESTIONS

1. Describe how the pattern of competition in a firm's industry affects the strategic planning process for international information systems.

2. At what stage in the evolution of the multinational enterprise should senior management begin planning for its international information resources?

3. Describe the major attributes of planning in the international versus the domestic environment.

4. Identify the major phases of the strategic planning process for international information systems and the objectives of each phase.

5. How do host country governments influence the strategic planning process for a multinational corporation's international information systems resources?

SUGGESTED READINGS

American Management Association. *International Management Information Systems: Approaches to Design and Implementation.* Management Bulletin No. 103. New York: American Management Association, 1967.

Bartlett, C. A., and S. Ghosal. "Managing Across Borders: New Strategic Requirements." *Sloan Management Review* (Fall 1987): 43–53.

Brandt, W. K., and J. M. Hulbert. "Patterns of Communication in the Multinational Corporation: An Empirical Study." *Journal of International Business Studies* 7 (1976): 57–64.

Buss, Martin D. J. "Managing International Information Systems." *Harvard Business Review* (September–October 1982): 153–162.

Carlyle, R. E. "Managing IS at Multinationals." *Datamation* (March 1, 1988): 54–57.

———. "The Tomorrow Organization." *Datamation* (February 1, 1990): 22–29.

Freedman, David H. "Managing Information Systems at the Multinational." *Infosystems* (January 1985): 58–62.

Gibson, M. L. "Implementing a Corporatewide Information Strategy Through CASE." *Journal of Information Systems Management* (Summer 1990): 8–17.

Henderson, John C. "Plugging Into Strategic Partnerships: The Critical IS Connection." *Sloan Management Review* (Spring 1990): 7–18.

"The Incredible Shrinking Company." *The Economist* (December 15, 1990): 65–66.

Ives, Blake, and Sirkka L. Jarvenpaa. "Applications of Global Information Technology: Key Issues for Management." *MIS Quarterly* (March 1991): 33–49.

Keen, Peter G. W. *An International Perspective on Managing Information Technologies.* Washington, DC: The International Center for Information Technologies, 1987.

Kneitel, A. M. "Evolving and Implementing a Worldwide Management Information System (IMS/MIS)." *MIS Quarterly* (September 1980): 31–40.

Levitt, T. "The Globalization of Markets." *Harvard Business Review* (May–June 1988): 92–102.

Management of Computer Resources in Multinational Corporations. Report No. M19. New York: The Diebold Group, Inc., 1970.

Multinational Computer Networks. Report No. T27. New York: The Diebold Group, Inc., 1973.

Murray, J. A. "Intelligence Systems of the MNCs." *Columbia Journal of World Business* 13 (1978): 19–26.

Nanus, Burt. "Business, Government and the Multinational Computer." *Columbia Journal of World Business* (Spring 1978): 19–26.

Ohmae, Kenichi. "Managing in a Borderless World." *Harvard Business Review* (May–June 1989): 152–161.

Porter, Michael E. "Changing Patterns of International Competition." *California Management Review* 2 (Winter 1986): 9–40.

Reck, R. H. "The Shock of Going Global." *Datamation* (August 1, 1989): 67–69.

Rubenstein, Albert H. *Managing Technology in the Decentralized Firm.* New York: Wiley-Interscience, Inc., 1989.

Selig, G. J. "A Framework for Multinational Information Systems Planning." *Information and Management* 5 (June 1982): 95–115.

——. "Approaches to Strategic Planning for Information Resource Management in Multinational Corporations." *MIS Quarterly* (June 1982): 33–45.

——. *Strategic Planning for Information Resource Management: A Multinational Perspective.* Ann Arbor, Michigan: UMI Research Press, 1983.

Tricker, R. I. "Information Resource Management—A Cross Cultural Perspective." *Information and Management* 15 (1988): 37–46.

Von Glinow, Mary Ann. *The New Professionals: Managing Today's High-Tech Employees.* Massachusetts: Ballinger, 1988.

Chapter S E V E N

Information Technology: Achieving Global Competitive Advantage

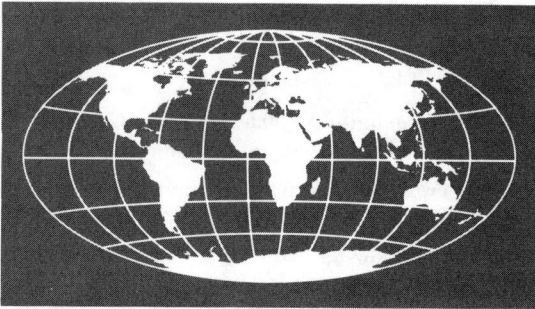

The efficient and innovative application of the latest technology has always been a source of competitive advantage in business. In the early days of America's expansion westward, the Pony Express was the most sophisticated information network for carrying messages and documents across the United States, taking only two or three weeks. However, with the invention of the telegraph and the development of a coast-to-coast transmission system, the Pony Express became obsolete almost overnight. Today, the telegraph has been replaced by the airplanes and trucks of firms such as Federal Express, a company completely designed and organized around the two key resources of information and technology.

Using sophisticated tracking and scheduling systems, hand-held data entry devices, large mainframe computers, and satellite communications, Federal Express can collect, sort, and deliver a package between any two points in the continental United States overnight. Even more amazing is the extension of the service to include overseas express services. Yet, even this leading-edge information technology is losing its competitive advantage as hundreds of thousands of desktop facsimile machines send and receive documents and images within minutes, and for less money.

Strategic information systems (SIS) are being implemented by a growing number of corporations. In fact, it is not uncommon for these applications to be proudly discussed in corporate annual reports, magazine and television ads, and other company literature. Satellites that once tracked the movement of military weaponry in the Soviet Union are now used by Toyota Motor Corporation to track the maintenance records of its Lexus owners anywhere in the world.

As we will discuss in this chapter, SIS extend beyond the simple automation of manual procedures and management decision support systems. Strategic information systems support and shape the firm's global competitive strategy. Information technology is increasingly being used as a competitive weapon to create market entry barriers, which prevent competition from gaining market share; extend and augment product offerings; differentiate firm services; and create switching costs, which make it inconvenient to change suppliers. In this chapter we will discuss the role and application of information technology and strategic information systems in multinational enterprises.

DEFINING STRATEGIC INFORMATION TECHNOLOGY SYSTEMS

In corporate boardrooms and executive offices all around the world, information systems are as much a part of the discussions as are strategies, long-range plans, and market-share goals. Clearly, one cannot avoid the topic in the popular business literature or in the daily conduct of business. But, what is information technology (IT) and what role does it have in firms competing on an international level?

Information technology can be defined simply as technology that combines hardware, software, and data components into an application that has strategic importance to the company. As presented in Figure

7–1, some researchers have viewed information technology as having an impact on three levels: the industry, the firm, and the firm's strategy. At the industry level, the application of information technology by a firm can change the products, services, markets, and production economics associated with that industry. For example, the backbone of the travel industry is a highly computerized travel agency network. Computerized reservation systems built by United Airlines and American Airlines in the 1970s to automate their own reservation processes are

---

Industry Level

Information technology changes an industry's:
- Products and services
- Markets
- Production economics

Firm Level

Information technology affects key competitive forces:
- Buyers
- Suppliers
- Substitution
- New entrants
- Rivalry

Strategy Level

Information technology affects a firm's strategy:
- Low-cost leadership
- Product differentiation
- Concentration on product/market niche

FIGURE 7–1   The Three-Level Impact of Information Technology

Source: Reprinted from "Information Technology: A New Competitive Weapon" by Gregory L. Parsons, *Sloan Management Review* (Fall, 1983): 4, by permission of the publisher. Copyright 1983 by the Sloan Management Review Association. All rights reserved.

now being used by 80 percent of the nation's 20,000 travel agencies, accounting for 90 percent of all airline ticket sales.[1] The presidents of these airlines readily acknowledge that everything they do comes from a computer. The lifeblood of business is information and those who harness it effectively gain a competitive advantage. Information technology also affects key competitive forces at the firm level. To understand these competitive forces, Michael Porter developed a framework that focuses on five basic competitive forces: buyers, suppliers, substitutes, new entrants, and firm rivalry.[2] Information technology applied at this level affects the firm's position within the industry through these competitive forces.[3] For example, General Motors is implementing an electronic data interchange (EDI) system for its parts suppliers located throughout Europe. In order to sell parts to any of GM's assembly facilities in Europe, the parts supplier must have compatible computer systems and accompanying shipping and invoicing systems to interface with GM. Prospective entrants into the industry must make a substantial investment in information technology to become a GM supplier. Thus, EDI systems become an entry barrier.

At the third level, information technology can affect a firm's strategy in one of three ways. First, information technology can contribute to a low-cost strategy. For example, Equitable Life Insurance uses an on-line inventory control and purchasing system to tie its field offices, regional offices, and corporate headquarters to four warehouses that stock office supplies such as paper clips, stationery, and pens. The system enables purchasing agents to analyze the total consumption of the firm's office supplies and negotiate with vendors for volume discounts for the entire company instead of for individual offices. As a result, Equitable reduced its operating costs by $2 million a year. Second, the firm may choose a strategy based on differentiation of its products. Information technology can be imbedded in the product or service or used in a way that clearly distinguishes products that have similar end uses. For example, GE's 24-hour, 365-day-a-year information service answers consumers' questions about the operation of its appliance products. Third, information technology can assist a firm following a market niche strategy by erecting entry barriers to prevent competition from gaining market share. A common application may include installation of a firm's customized software on personal computers and placing the computers in a customer's office. For example, Builder's Mart of America (BMA) provides small, family-owned hardware stores with personal computers to control inventory. The system also makes it easy to submit small-volume orders to BMA, which in turn pools these orders and buys directly from the manufacturer, resulting in a captive market niche benefiting both the store owner and Builder's Mart.

We have shown how information technology can affect the industry, the firm, and the firm's strategy. We will now discuss the attributes that make an information system strategic to the enterprise.

STRATEGIC INFORMATION SYSTEMS

Information technology becomes a tool for gaining a competitive advantage when it is used to shape or directly support the competitive strategy of the firm.[4] Figure 7–2 presents the major differences between information technology applied in traditional management information systems (MIS), management support systems (MSS), and strategic information systems (SIS). As the figure shows, information technology applied in MIS focuses primarily on transaction processing such as accounting and

Use / Function	Automate Basic Processes	Satisfy Information Needs	Enhance Competitive Strategy
Transactions	MIS		SIS
Query and Analysis		MSS	SIS

FIGURE 7–2 Varieties of Information Systems

Source: Charles Wiseman, *Strategy and Computers* (Homewood, IL: Dow Jones-Irwin, 1985), p. 231.

payroll systems. MIS automate manual procedures related to the daily operations of the organization. On the other hand, through MSS, information technology is applied to satisfy the information needs of managers. Typically, these systems enable ad hoc query and analysis of historical databases to support the firm's decision-making process. At another level, SIS apply information technology as a competitive tool or weapon. SIS can have a dual strategic emphasis, either directly *supporting* or *shaping* the firm's strategy. For example, information technology supported Merril Lynch's strategy in the creation of the Cash Management Account, which offers its customers the benefits of checking, credit cards, and money-market funds in one package. SIS shaped Federal Express's strategy in the use of hand-held data entry devices to accurately track the collection, transit, and delivery of packages.

Strategic IT Questions

To assess the competitive potential of strategic information systems, some researchers suggest that management address five key questions.[5]

1. Can information systems build barriers to entry that prevent or discourage competition for the firm's product or market?

2. Can information systems build switching costs such that customers will have to spend too much time and money to change suppliers?

3. Can information technology shift the basis of competition to either a low cost, product differentiation or a market-niche orientation?

4. Can information technology change the balance of power in a firm's supplier relationships and thus dictate better terms?

5. Can information technology generate new products and services for the firm?

Extending an investment in SIS to the international environment has become a critical issue for firms competing in global industries and considering expansion into international markets. Are the same questions and issues outlined above valid for enterprises competing in international markets? If so, can firms with overseas manufacturing and marketing subsidiaries transfer their information technology abroad? The simple answer to these questions is yes. However, the international environment presents a set of economic and noneconomic factors that create a very complex business domain that must be thoroughly understood to effectively implement strategic information systems in multinational enterprises.

Global IT Platforms

Information technology that can be applied in multiple business environments around the world forms what can be described as *global information technology platforms*. Global information technology platforms enable multinational enterprises to use information and systems internally or externally to gain a competitive advantage over indigenous host country firms that have extensive local market knowledge. Essentially, information technology assists the foreign enterprise in overcoming the home-court advantage of local firms in the host country. Sophisticated information systems developed in one country such as the United States can be transferred to overseas subsidiaries where they can be adapted to the local country environment, giving the subsidiary immediate advantages.

Global Strategic Imperatives and Information Technology

Up to this point we have been discussing the use of information technology with limited reference to the international business environment or global competition. In this section we will examine the application of information technology to gain a competitive advantage in the international environment. Firms competing in the international marketplace are faced with a dual imperative that is reflected in the slogan "think global, act local." Figure 7–3 presents the primary factors driving the dual imperative.[6]

The imperative that multinational corporations be responsive to the national environment stems from the diversity of national markets and the demands placed on the enterprise by the host country government. National differences are manifested in market structures, industry structures, distribution channels, manufacturing processes, and customer needs. Host government demands reflect the need for control over the foreign company to protect the sovereignty of the nation-state and its indigenous industries.

The imperative that multinational corporations integrate their operation into a one-world organization is driven by the fact that these enterprises must service their customers in many countries while meeting

NATIONAL RESPONSIVENESS	GLOBAL INTEGRATION
The Dual Imperative	

Diversity among national markets in:
  Market structures
  Industry structures
  Distribution channels
  Manufacturing process
  Customer needs
	Multinational customers
	Global competitors
	High technology
	Scale and experience in manufacturing

Host government demands:
  Norms and standards
  Trade barriers
  Importance of public
    sector market
  Regulation of MNC
    activity
	Investment intensity and access to raw materials and energy
	Universal product needs

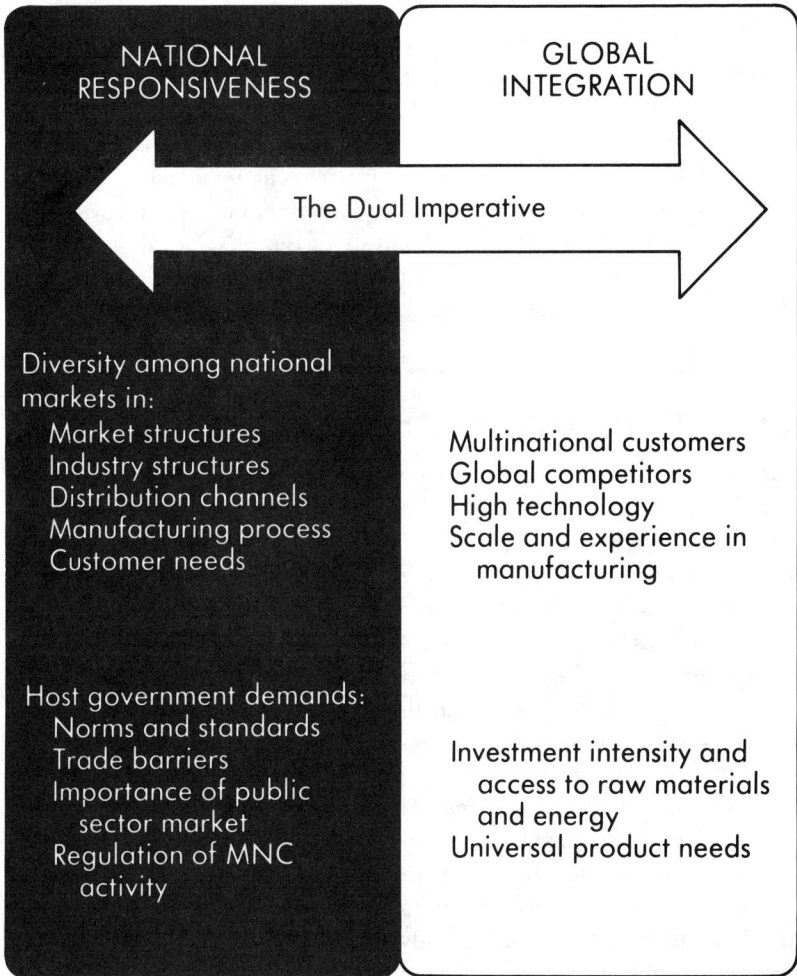

FIGURE 7-3   Factors Contributing to National Responsiveness and Global Integration
Source: Yves Doz and C. K. Prahalad, "Patterns of Strategic Control within Multinational Corporations," *Journal of International Business Studies* (Fall 1984): 56.

global competition in every market. For example, IBM sells computers to General Motors in many countries while competing against the Japanese computer manufacturers Hitachi and NEC in each of these markets. Given the high cost of research and development, IBM must produce products requiring little adaptation that can be marketed in all countries.

Essentially, the dual imperative requires the multinational enterprise to balance the need to operate on a country-by-country basis by adapting their products, operations, and policies to a national level, with the need to achieve advantages of scale and scope that result from integration of its operations on a global scale without regard to national boundaries. Information technology can be a critical success factor in achieving global competitive advantage if the firm uses its information systems investment to address the dual imperative. Analysis of the MNC's value activities in relation to the information demands of national responsiveness and global integration provides the means for identifying SIS opportunities.

THE GLOBAL VALUE CHAIN APPROACH TO SIS

Business executives in all countries continuously search for new ways of achieving sustainable competitive advantage for their firms. The value chain approach advocated by Michael Porter has become a standard framework for analyzing a firm and its competition to find ways of creating competitive advantage.[7] This framework can be used by MIS executives to identify ways in which information can create competitive advantage. Figure 7–4 illustrates the relationship among three types of information systems and the primary and support activities of the firm's value chain.

Both domestic firms and multinational corporations possess a generic value chain structure consisting of five primary activities that include inbound logistics, operations, outbound logistics, marketing and sales, and service; and four accompanying support activities including procurement, technology development, human resource management, and firm infrastructure. Competitive advantage is gained when these activities are organized and conducted in a manner that puts the firm in one of three relative positions: (1) low-cost producer/marketer, (2) firm/product differentiation, or (3) secure market niche (focus). Information systems that shape or support these value activities are considered strategic information systems because of their potential impact on the firm's competitive position.

A major difference in the application of strategic information systems to domestic and multinational enterprises is related to the international coordination and configuration of the value chain activities. In purely domestic enterprises, all of the value activities are conducted in a single-

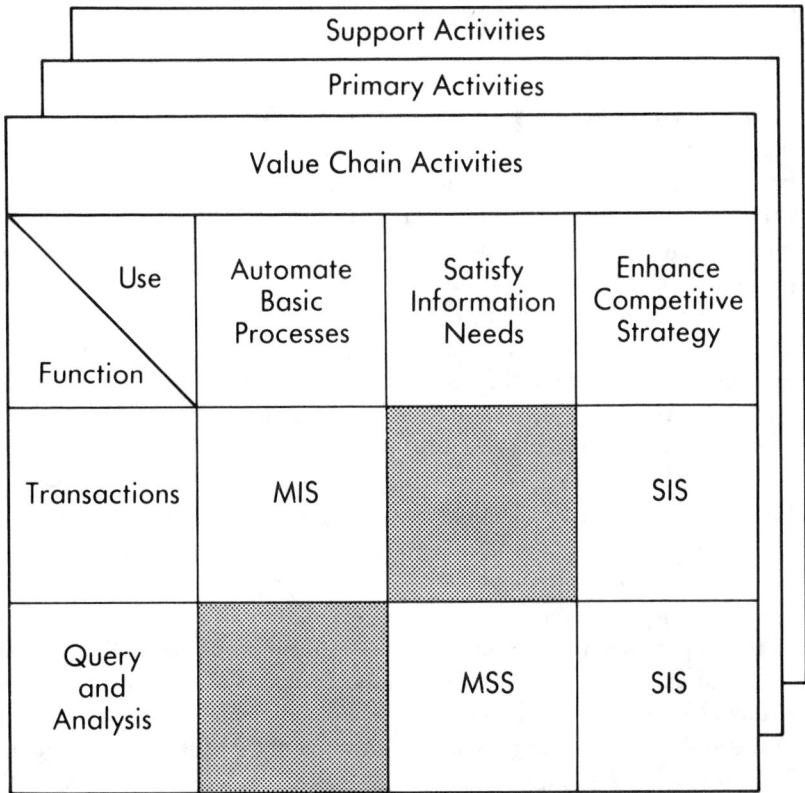

FIGURE 7-4 Value Chain Approach to Information Systems

country domain. In a multinational enterprise, the value activities are spread across many nations, making coordination a major managerial task. The key considerations in formulating a global strategy essentially involve where the firm conducts the value chain activities and how it coordinates them across national boundaries. To identify how information systems can be used to gain competitive advantage, a key concern focuses on the way information technology can be used to enhance the coordination of the firm's value activities relative to the competition. The starting point for this assessment is to determine the nature of the firm's international competition. Does the firm compete in a multidomestic industry environment or a global industry environment?

STRATEGIC INFORMATION SYSTEMS IN MULTIDOMESTIC INDUSTRIES

International companies compete in industries that lie along a continuum that is multidomestic at one end and global at the other.[8] The distinguishing difference between multidomestic and global industries is the competition that occurs within the industry. In a multidomestic industry, the competitive forces in one country do not affect the nature of competition in another. Strategy formulation takes place on a country-by-country basis in which the firm's international operations are viewed as a portfolio of subsidiaries. The firm's strategy is country-centered and managed as a portfolio. Figure 7–5 illustrates the firm's information systems environment with a multidomestic perspective.

In the multidomestic environment, an enterprise can gain a competitive advantage from one-time transfers of knowledge and technology. Information systems applications developed in one country can be transferred to other countries. For example, an inventory control system developed in the United States can be transferred as a whole or adapted to meet the needs of the firm's foreign subsidiaries. Because the expense of developing such a system has already been incurred by the parent organization, the cost to the overseas subsidiary is very low. The operational savings of the system may enable the subsidiary to lower its prices and achieve greater market penetration in the host country market. Until the system is duplicated by other local competitors, the firm will enjoy a competitive advantage from this one-time information technology transfer.

In a multidomestic industry environment, the multinational corporation can gain a competitive advantage in each host country by evaluating the potential impact of transferring information systems developed in one country to other countries. But, competitive advantage is not gained only by transfer of strategic information systems. In a multidomestic industry environment, competitive advantage can also be gained through MIS and MSS applications. Even a simple application system such as accounting can provide an advantage in countries where accounting procedures are still performed manually. But the system can provide an advantage only if it lowers the cost of performing the overall accounting function. Information technology transfer is the vehicle for achieving competitive advantage in this environment.

Country managers using management support systems for query and analysis can contribute to the competitive position of the subsidiaries if

	Automate Basic Processes	Satisfy Information Needs	Enhance Competitive Strategy
Transactions	MIS		SIS
Query and Analysis		MSS	SIS

Value Chain Activities

Use / Function

U.S.A.
Japan
Germany
Brazil

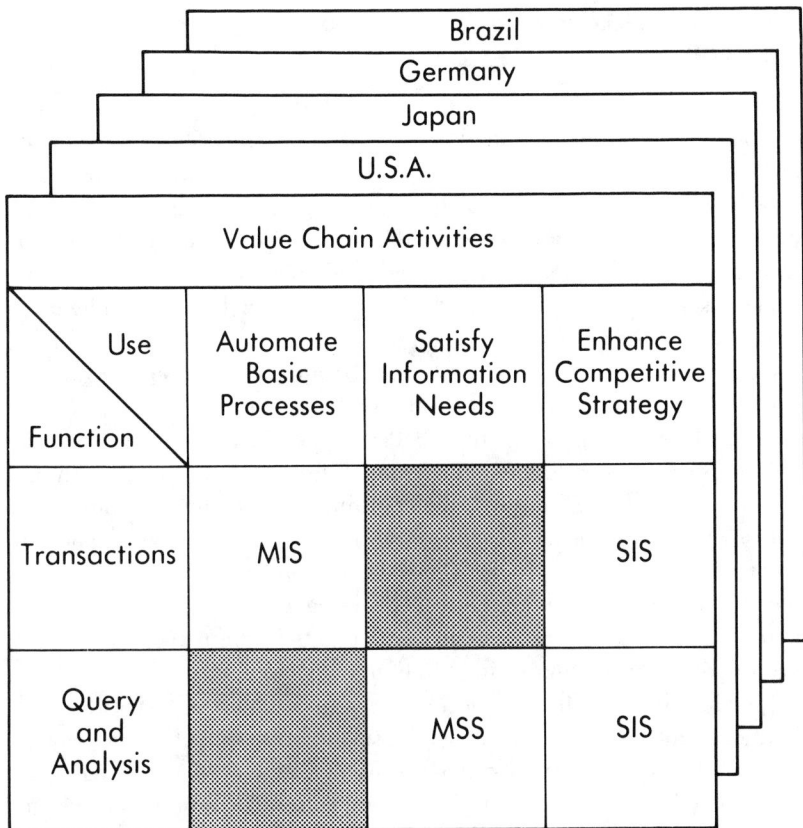

FIGURE 7-5   Information Systems in Multidomestic Industries

using the systems developed by the parent corporation leads them to make local business decisions that are better than those of managers in competing local enterprises. The same is true for strategic information systems that shape or support the firm's strategy in the local country market.

Because competitive forces do not cross national borders in a multidomestic industry, a firm can gain significant competitive advantage from its value activities by focusing its strategic information systems "downstream" on the buyer or customer. Information systems that create entry or mobility barriers or that differentiate the firm's products and services contribute substantially to the firms competitive advantage in multidomestic industry environments.

STRATEGIC INFORMATION SYSTEMS IN GLOBAL INDUSTRIES

Global industries present a set of competitive forces quite different from multidomestic industries. In global industries, competition in one country has an impact on a firm's competitive position in other countries. A good example of a global industry is the computer industry. IBM competes against Japanese, French, and German computer manufacturers in every country. Because these global competitors have access to the same resources around the world, IBM does not have an indigenous advantage in any one country. Gaining a competitive advantage in global industries requires the firm to view its operation as an integrated whole. Thus, the enterprise strategy is not country specific.

The firm's goals are achieved through a global strategy based on either low-cost production or product differentiation. Strategy implementation is achieved through the coordination and configuration of the firm's value chain, where it will locate its activities worldwide, and how these value activities will be coordinated. For example, a global firm may locate manufacturing facilities in low-wage-rate countries to support a low-cost strategy, or it may locate its plants in the market in which it sells to achieve product differentiation.

Unlike in a multidomestic industry, in a global industry the multinational enterprise will rarely gain a sustainable competitive advantage from its MIS or MSS application portfolio. These systems can easily be duplicated by the competition. It is through strategic information systems that global competitors can gain an advantage. Multinational corporations competing in global industries take either a triadic approach or a global approach to organizing and managing their investment in information systems. Figure 7-6 illustrates a triadic perspective in global industries.

The triadic approach is typical of most multinational corporations. Using this approach, the firm formulates a strategy without respect to geography and implements that strategy through regional organizations. The firm's value added activities are configured and coordinated on a regional basis. Typically, regional blocks such as North and South America, Asia, and Europe become the organizing typology. Information systems are also organized on this basis to coincide with the location of the firm's value chain activities.

Application of information technology using a triadic approach has two advantages. First, information systems developed and implemented in one region such as Europe can be transferred to other regions. Unlike

Europe

Asia

Americas

Value Chain Activities

Function \ Use	Automate Basic Processes	Satisfy Information Needs	Enhance Competitive Strategy
Transactions	MIS		SIS
Query and Analysis		MSS	SIS

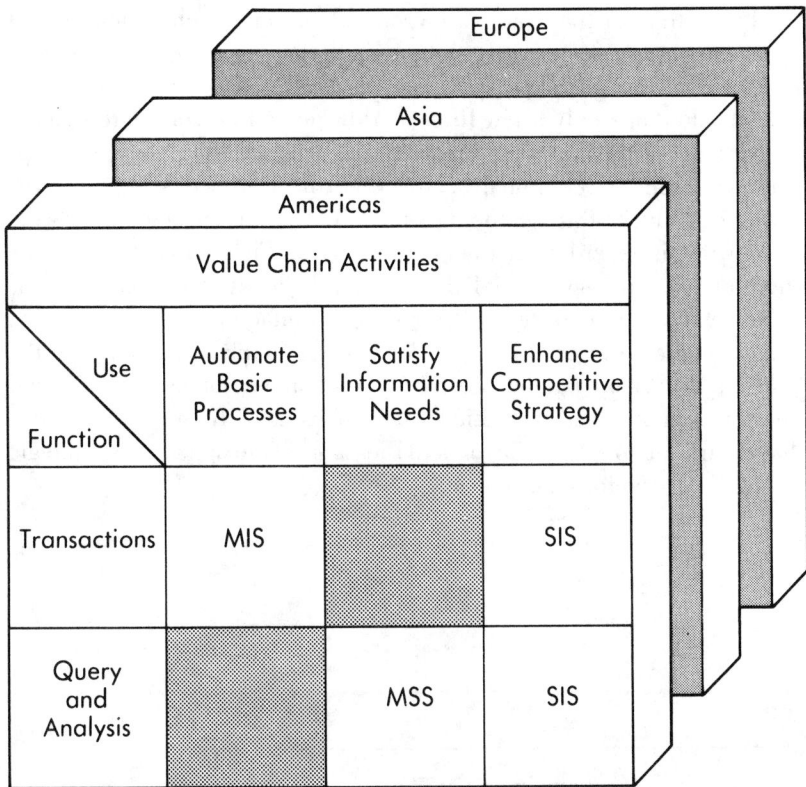

FIGURE 7-6 Information Systems in the Global Environment from a Triadic Perspective

in a multidomestic industry, the advantages gained from the transfer of information technology are small and result from market imperfections in the cost of developing information systems in each region. Second, the triadic approach enables the multinational corporation to balance the dual imperative by being somewhat responsive to individual country requirements while integrating its operations on a regional basis. As a result of the triadic approach, strategic information systems in one region may vary substantially from those in other regions. For example, a multinational corporation may employ information technology in Europe to create entry barriers, while pursuing information systems development strategies in Asia that affect its supplier relationships.

In contrast to the triadic view, the global approach organizes and views the enterprise activities from a single-market perspective. Figure 7–7 presents this global perspective with regard to the firm's information systems. Perhaps only a few firms worldwide can be considered global enterprises by the way they organize and manage their worldwide operations. From a true global perspective, the firm seeks to gain competitive advantage through the integration of its activities on a worldwide scale without regard to national boundaries. Firms operating in this environment have substantial investments in many countries with numerous value activities such as research, manufacturing, and marketing being conducted in each country. How to rationalize and maximize the firm's resources on a global scale becomes a major concern for the firm. There is less of a focus on national responsiveness. Information systems that contribute to integration of activities worldwide are seen as strategic by the firm's senior management.

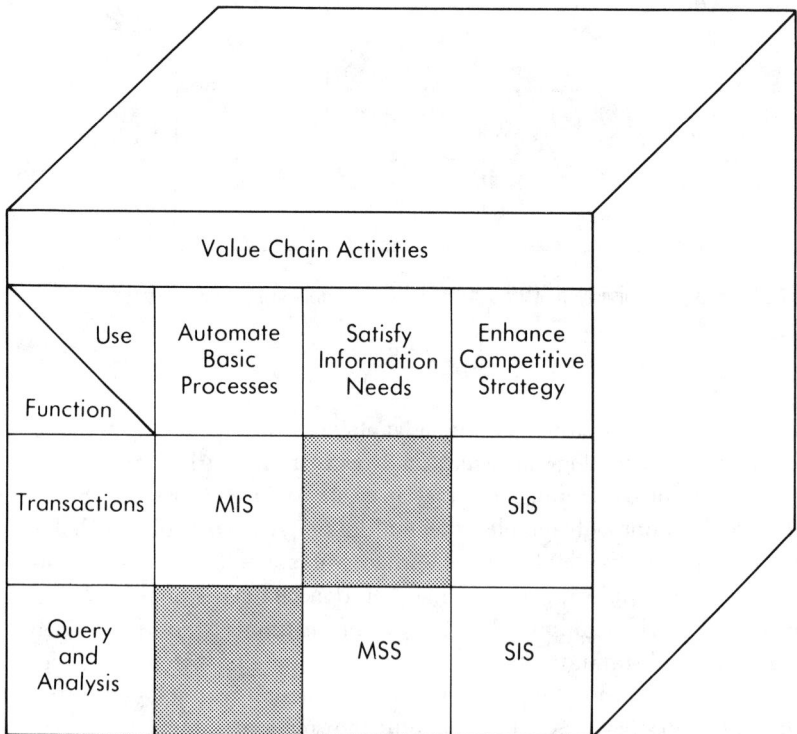

Value Chain Activities			
Use ⟍ Function	Automate Basic Processes	Satisfy Information Needs	Enhance Competitive Strategy
Transactions	MIS		SIS
Query and Analysis		MSS	SIS

FIGURE 7–7   Information Systems in the Global Industry Environment

In global industry environments, competitive advantage is gained by focusing "upstream" on the firm's suppliers. Competitive advantage is achieved quite differently in multidomestic industries than in global industries. Therefore, the role of information technology is also different. In the next section we discuss the role of strategic information systems by exploring the concept of strategic thrusts.

STRATEGIC THRUSTS AND INFORMATION TECHNOLOGY

In his book, *Strategy and Computers*, Charles Wiseman describes five strategic thrusts in which information systems can play an offensive or defensive role in establishing a sustainable competitive position for the firm.[9] The thrusts include differentiation, cost, innovation, growth, and alliance. Figure 7–8 presents the multidomestic and global industry environments in which the thrusts can be implemented. The environment where each thrust is pursued using information systems varies, depending on whether the industry is multidomestic or global in structure. In the following discussion, we will define and discuss each strategic thrust and then we will examine the impact of each thrust using information technology in multidomestic and global environments.

Differentiation. Information systems can be used to differentiate the firm's product in one of three ways: (1) by changing various elements of the marketing mix such as delivery time, quantity, and terms of the sale, (2) by enhancing the marketing support system, and (3) by extending the product to meet other customer needs. Strategic information systems in the international environment can be used as a market entry tool. For example, the large Japanese cosmetics manufacturer, Shiseido, provides each of its retail outlets with a computer system that enables cosmetologists to analyze a customer's skin, simulate the results of using Shiseido products, and provide an individually tailored, cosmetic-use program. By using a strategic information system to support the firm's market entry strategy, Shiseido was able to capture a significant market share in relatively little time.

Cost. Two major areas that contribute significantly to cost reduction include economies of scale and economies of scope. Firms gain a competitive advantage through strategic cost thrusts by reducing or avoiding costs in their internal operations or by increasing the competition's cost of doing business. Cost reduction and cost avoidance extend beyond the firm to include the firm's suppliers and customers.

Economies of scale are related to two dimensions in international

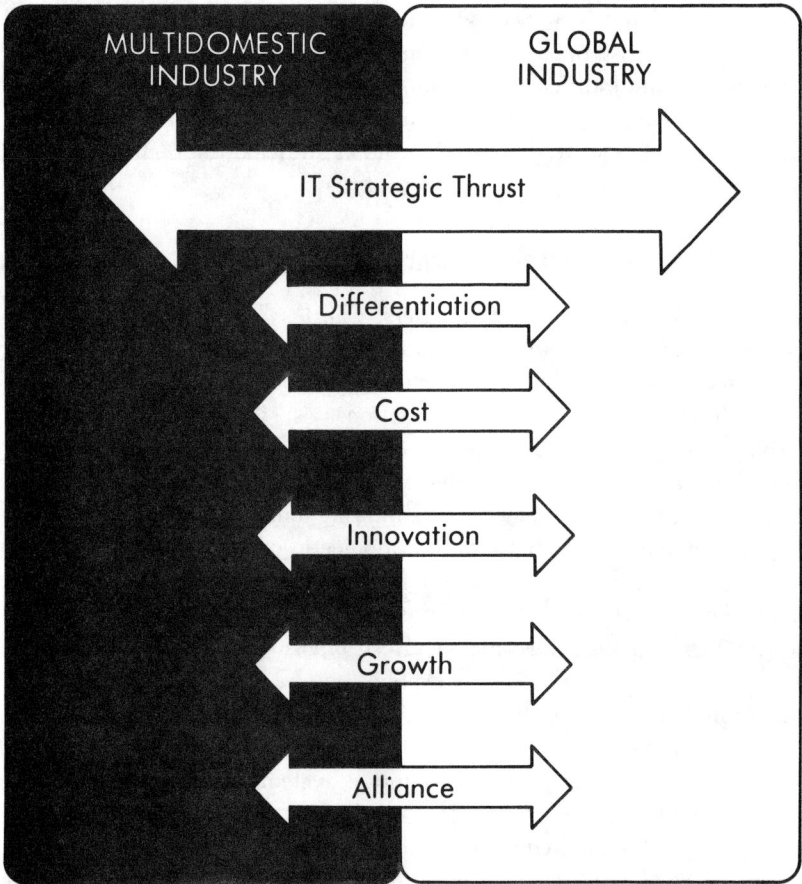

FIGURE 7 – 8   Information Technology: Strategic Thrusts in Multidomestic and Global Industry Environments

business: coordination and configuration. Economies of scale are achieved through improved coordination of the firm's value activities or through the concentration or dispersion (configuration) of the firm's value activities around the world. For example, the labor-intensive components of a manufactured product may be produced in relatively low-wage-rate countries, while the capital-intensive components are produced in technologically rich countries. Final assembly of the components is done in the country where the product is to be marketed. A multiplant production system achieves increased economies of scale but requires a high level of coordination among the plant sites.

Economies of scope, the second area of a strategic cost thrust where computers can be a factor, occur through the combination of two or more processes or products. For example, Toyota builds several different car models on the same manufacturing line. By eliminating the need for additional manufacturing lines, Toyota is able to lower its per unit cost of manufacturing. The same economies of scope can involve strategic information systems. Japan Airlines uses excess capacity in its passenger reservation systems to book sporting events throughout Japan. The additional revenue enables JAL to reduce the per unit cost of ticketing its passengers.

Innovation. A strategic innovation thrust gives a firm an advantage over its competitors or reduces the competitors' advantages. Innovation is two fold. First, it refers to product innovations developed by discovering previously unmet customer needs. Second, innovation refers to the design and adoption of new processes that increase the value added to a firm's product or service in the value chain. When information is a key component of innovation, information systems become the tool for implementing the strategic thrust. For example, when IBM Japan needed to expand its downtown Tokyo offices to accommodate an increase in its sales force, the high cost of real estate prevented IBM from justifying the required expansion of its sales offices. The solution was to use an information system to more effectively manage the firm's existing office space. No longer would marketing representatives have their own desks. When salespeople returned to the IBM office, they would log onto the office information system, locate an empty desk, and assign themselves to the desk. The system would automatically forward their telephone calls and allow the marketing managers to know how much time the salespeople spent in the office. Because at any given time, only 40 to 50 percent of the sales force would be in the office, each person would be given a portable storage cabinet that could be stored when the person was out of the office or rolled to the assigned desk location when necessary. IBM gained a competitive advantage by expanding its sales force without incurring the additional fixed costs of new office space.

Growth. Strategic growth thrusts are similar in many ways to differentiation. Growth thrusts occur in three areas: product, function, and spin-offs. Product growth refers to the ability of the firm to expand its product line with new models and features that better meet the needs of segmented target markets. For example, the Sony Walkman has grown from one model to over 20 different models to meet the diverse needs of people who want specific features such as AM/FM radio, water-resistance, or light-weight cases.

Growth in function relates to the value chain activities of forward and backward integration. For example, a firm may merge with its major raw materials supplier or expand its distribution network through the acquisition of independent retail outlets. Strategic information systems enable the firm to take advantage of these new linkages by reducing costs and information float.

The third area in a strategic growth thrust is spin-offs. Spin-offs are new business organizations created within the firm's value chain. For example, GE has undertaken a program called "work out" in which the firm identifies value activities that it can spin off into separate business organizations. One work-out program involved business travel. GE established its own travel department because of the volume of travel that GE management generated on a yearly basis. After several years, GE established the department as a separate travel business available to GE personnel and the general public. Now GE has the advantages of reduced travel costs for its managers and a new revenue generator for the firm.

Alliances. A strategic alliance is a thrust that is often used as a tool for implementing one of the other strategic thrusts. A firm pursues an alliance when it does not have the resources or expertise to undertake a particular strategic thrust by itself. Pursuit of alliances is a growing activity in international business. Even large multinational corporations such as GM, IBM, and Toyota have entered into strategic alliances for the purpose of differentiation, innovation, growth, and cost reduction. The alliance enables the firm to expand its product line or enhance its value chain activities. A strategic alliance can take one of three basic forms: joint venture, acquisition, or formal agreement.

An excellent example of a strategic alliance involves the automobile parts industries in Japan and the United States. For many years U.S. parts suppliers have tried without success to supply Japanese original equipment manufacturers (OEMs) such as Toyota, Honda, and Nissan. While Japanese OEMs continue to build new U.S. manufacturing facilities, Japanese and American parts manufacturers are establishing joint ventures that combine U.S. distribution and marketing capability with Japanese quality and manufacturing technology. These alliances will survive as long as each partner gains an advantage from the strategic thrust.

Strategic information systems can be used to support and shape any or all of the five strategic thrusts—differentiation, cost, innovation, growth, and alliance. The objective of the strategic thrust and its accompanying information system is to either increase the firm's competitive advantage or decrease its disadvantage. While the technical application of a strategic information system is the same for domestic and international enterprises, the environment (global versus multidomestic) in which the system is implemented has a potential impact on the effectiveness of the strategic thrust. In the next section we discuss the implications of these strategic thrusts in multidomestic and global industry environments.

STRATEGIC OPPORTUNITY IN MULTIDOMESTIC AND GLOBAL INDUSTRIES

A global strategy addresses two dimensions of an international value chain: how the firm will coordinate its value activities that span multiple countries and where these value added activities will be located (configuration).[10] Figure 7–9 presents a typology of multidomestic and global industry environments according to their coordination and configuration dimensions. As the figure shows, multidomestic industry environments are characterized by value chain activities that are concentrated in single

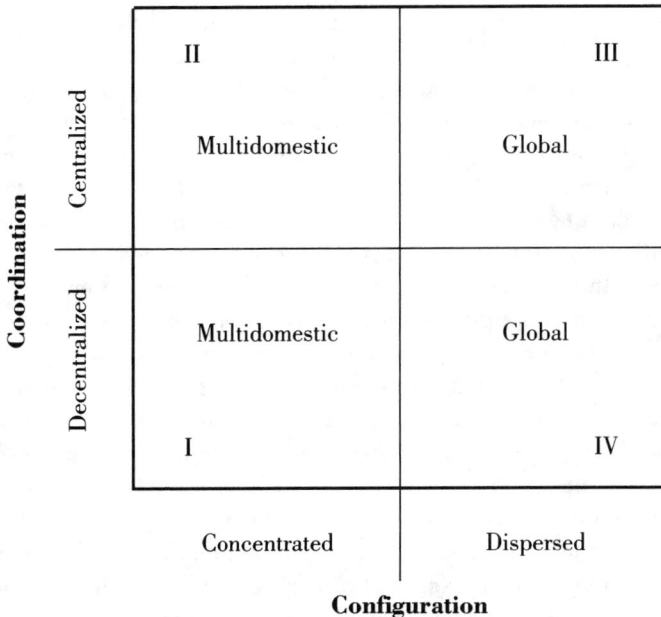

FIGURE 7-9 A Typology of the International Business Environment

countries. The firm operating in a multidomestic environment can co-ordinate its value activities using a centralized or decentralized managerial approach. In contrast, global industry environments include firms that have value chain activities that are dispersed across many countries. These activities can also be coordinated in a decentralized or centralized manner. For example, IBM operates in the quadrant-IV environment while McDonalds operates in quadrant I, with single-country value chains that are decentralized.

In assessing the potential impact of each of the five strategic thrusts using information technology, it is important for management to understand that each strategic thrust has a multidomestic and a global dimension. The potential impact is dependent on the industry environment in which the strategic thrust is implemented.

Multinational corporations implement strategic thrusts to achieve different goals depending on whether the industry environment is multidomestic or global. When strategic information systems are used to support or shape these strategic thrusts, the potential impact varies by industry environment. The potential impact of strategic information systems in the firm's strategic thrust is two fold. The use of information technology can have an impact on the competitive marketplace or it can focus on the firm's internal operations. While the end result of deploying information technology in a strategic thrust is to achieve a competitive advantage or reduce a competitive disadvantage, the primary impact of the information technology application is either internal—on the firm's operations—or external—in the marketplace. Figure 7–10 presents the primary impact of information technology for each of the five strategic thrusts according to the industry environment in which it is implemented.

Strategic information systems in each industry environment can affect one of three areas: the competitive marketplace, one or more value activities of the enterprise's internal operations, or both areas without favoring either one. As Figure 7–10 shows, there are twenty possible combinations of strategic information technology thrusts and industry environments. The matrix can be used to guide the firm's choice of strategic thrust based on the desired competitive impact—marketplace, internal operations, or both.

If the multinational corporation embarks on a strategic differentiation or alliance thrust, the primary impact for both multidomestic and global industry environments is similar. If the enterprise operates in a decentralized approach with a low level of coordination of its value activities, the primary impact of using strategic information systems to support or

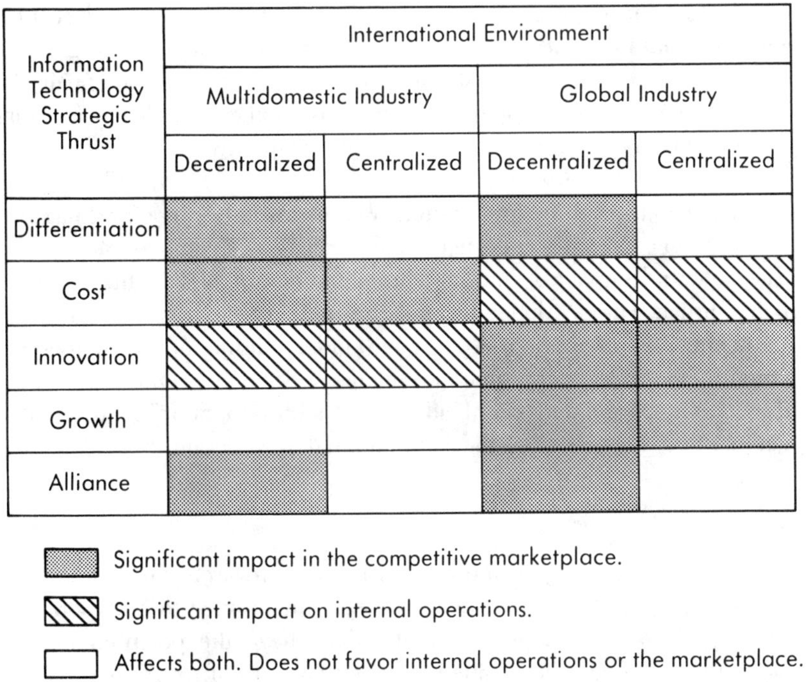

Information Technology Strategic Thrust	International Environment			
	Multidomestic Industry		Global Industry	
	Decentralized	Centralized	Decentralized	Centralized
Differentiation	�market		▮market	
Cost	▮market	▮market	▨internal	▨internal
Innovation	▨internal	▨internal	▮market	▮market
Growth			▮market	
Alliance	▮market		▮market	

▮ Significant impact in the competitive marketplace.

▨ Significant impact on internal operations.

☐ Affects both. Does not favor internal operations or the marketplace.

FIGURE 7-10   The Impact of Strategic Information System Thrusts in the International Environment

shape the strategic thrust is in the competitive marketplace. In contrast, if the multinational corporation is organized in a centralized manner, the impact of information technology does not favor internal operations or the marketplace, but may have an impact on both areas.

For multinational enterprises, a strategic cost or innovation thrust will have a different impact from the application of information technology, depending on whether the competition is in a multidomestic or global industry environment. A strategic cost thrust using information technology will primarily affect the competitive marketplace in a multidomestic environment and internal operations in a global industry environment. A strategic innovation thrust undertaken by the multinational enterprise will have an opposite effect. In a multidomestic environment, the impact is primarily focused on the firm's internal operations, while in a global industry environment it is focused on the competitive marketplace.

Unlike the strategic thrusts of differentiation/alliance and cost/innovation that have either the same or opposite effects depending on the industry environment, the strategic growth thrust does not favor the marketplace or internal operations in a multidomestic industry environment, and has a primary impact on the competitive marketplace in a global industry environment.

The manager of the information systems resources in a multinational corporation can employ information technology as a competitive weapon. The potential impact of information technology in each of the five strategic thrusts varies, depending on the industry environment in which the technology is applied. A thorough understanding of the competitive potential of strategic information systems and the environment in which they are implemented can lead to the achievement of a sustainable competitive advantage by the multinational corporation.

SUMMARY

Information technology combines hardware, software, and data components into applications that have strategic importance to a corporation. Strategic information systems applications have the potential to substantially influence the competitive position of the firm in its industry. These applications can affect the firm on one or more levels: industry, firm, and strategy. Today, multinational corporations seek ways to leverage their investment in information technology to gain a competitive advantage overseas.

A strategic information system both shapes and supports the firm's strategy. In the international environment management must recognize the key differences between the nature of competition in multidomestic and global industries. The benefits of SIS are different in each environment. Specifically, strategic information systems applications help a firm achieve competitive advantage in the international environment when they assist the firm in balancing the demands of the dual imperative— national responsiveness and global integration. National responsiveness stems from an awareness of differences in market and industry structure or the demands of host country governments. Global integration, the need to rationalize a firm's operations, is driven by technology, similar consumer needs, and economies of scale.

We discussed the concept of using a global or triadic approach to strategic information systems. The triadic view of the world divides the firm's operations into three geographic areas: Europe, the Americas, and Asia. Competitive advantage is achieved through one-time transfers of technology among these regional operations. In contrast, a global perspective leads a firm to develop information systems without regard to national or regional differences. The firm will organize and manage the development of these systems, depending on its approach.

We also discussed the application of information technology in the form of a strategic thrust. Strategic thrusts include differentiation, cost, innovation, growth, and alliance. Each of these five strategic thrusts can affect one of two areas: the competitive marketplace or internal operations. The impact of these strategic thrusts is dependent on whether the industry environment is multidomestic or global. Firms that successfully achieve sustainable competitive advantage in the international environment understand these differences and use strategic information systems technology accordingly.

NOTES

1. Various corporate annual reports.

2. Michael E. Porter, *Competitive Strategy* (New York: The Free Press, 1980).

3. Gregory L. Parsons, "Information Technology: A New Competitive Weapon," *Sloan Management Review* (Fall 1983): 5–6.

4. Charles Wiseman, *Strategy and Computers* (Homewood, IL: Dow Jones-Irwin, 1985): 7.

5. F. Warren McFarlan, "Information Technology Changes the Way You Compete," *Harvard Business Review* (May–June 1984): 99–101.

6. Yves Doz and C. K. Prahalad, "Patterns of Strategic Control Within Multinational Corporations," *Journal of International Business Studies* (Fall 1984): 55–72.

7. Michael E. Porter, *Competitive Advantage* (New York: The Free Press, 1982).

8. Michael E. Porter, "Changing Patterns of International Competition," *California Management Review* (Winter 1986): 9–40.

9. Wiseman.

10. For an excellent discussion of this concept, see Porter, "Changing Patterns."

STUDY QUESTIONS

1. Explain the differences between management information systems, management support systems, and strategic information systems. What role does each have in multidomestic and global industry environments?

2. What is the dual imperative and how does it influence the information systems of a multinational corporation?

3. What are the competitive implications for a firm operating in a global versus a multidomestic industry environment?

4. Explain the concept of strategic thrusts.

5. Describe the role of strategic information systems in achieving competitive advantage in an international environment versus a domestic environment.

SUGGESTED READINGS

Bakos, J. Y., and M. E. Treacy. "Information Technology and Corporate Strategy." *MIS Quarterly* (June 1986): 107–119.

Bergeron, F., C. Buteau, and L. Raymond. "Identification of Strategic Information Systems Opportunities: Applying and Comparing Two Methodologies." *MIS Quarterly* (March 1991): 89–103.

Benjamin, Robert I., John F. Rockart, et al. "Information Technology: A Strategic Opportunity." *Sloan Management Review* (Spring 1984).

Cash, James I., and Benn R. Konsynski. "IS Redraws Competitive Boundaries." *Harvard Business Review* (March–April 1985).

Cheney, P. H., and G. W. Dickson. "Organizational Characteristics and Information Systems: An Exploratory Investigation." *Academy of Management Journal* (March 1982): 170–184.

Dennis, A. R., J. F. Nunamaker, D. Paranka, and D. R. Vogel. "A New Role for Computers in Strategic Management." *The Journal of Business Strategy* (September–October 1990): 38–43.

Gerstein, Marc, and Heather Reisman. "Creating Competitive Advantage with Computer Technology." *Journal of Business Strategy* (Summer 1982).

Lucas, Henry C., Jr., and Jon A. Turner. "A Corporate Strategy for the Control of Information Processing." *Sloan Management Review* (Spring 1982).

McFarlan, F. W. "Information Technology Changes the Way You Compete." *Harvard Business Review* (May–June 1984): 98–103.

Neo, Boon Siong. "Information Technology and Global Competition: A Framework for Analysis." *Information and Management* (Spring 1991): 151–160.

Parsons, G. L. "Information Technology: A New Competitive Weapon." *Sloan Management Review* (Fall 1983): 3–14.

Porter, Michael E. "Technology and Competitive Advantage." *The Journal of Business Strategy* (Winter 1985): 60–78.

———. "How Information Gives You Competitive Advantage." *Harvard Business Review* (July–August 1985): 149–160.

————. *Competition in Global Industries.* Boston: Harvard Business School Press, 1986.

————. *The Competitive Advantage of Nations.* New York: Free Press, 1990.

Rockart, J. F., and J. E. Short. "IT in the 1990s: Managing Organizational Interdependence." *Sloan Management Review* (Winter 1989): 7–17.

Steel, Lowell W. *Managing Technology: The Strategic View.* New York: McGraw-Hill, 1989.

Wiseman, C. *Strategic Information Systems.* Homewood, IL: Dow Jones-Irwin, 1988.

Yip, George S. "Global Strategy . . . in a World of Nations?" *Sloan Management Review* (Fall 1989): 29–41.

Chapter EIGHT

EMERGING GLOBAL INFORMATION SYSTEMS ISSUES

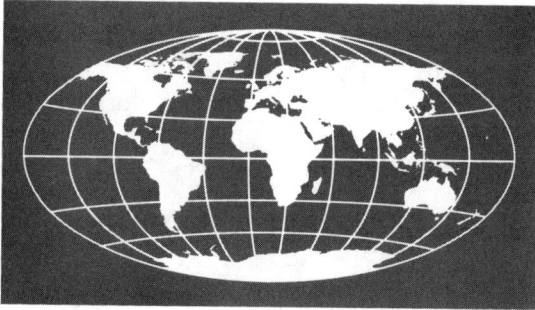

In Chapter 1 we described two major forces that are transforming the environment of business and the practice of management: the globalization of the marketplace and the impact of information technology on the firm. The link between these two forces is information. Information is power. It is economic power and it is managerial power.

Arno Penzias, vice president of research at AT&T Bell Laboratories, describes the evolution of the workplace: "As work becomes increasingly information intensive, I see organizational success depending more and more on giving each individual contributor needed information at the right place, at the right time, and in the right form. The degree to which this requirement can be met depends crucially on the information architecture used, the organization's nerve system."[1] In a global environment, this means that information must cross many barriers including time; geography; culture; and economic, legal, and political systems if it is to fulfill Penzias's requirement for organizational success. In this chapter we will examine the emerging global issues that affect the development and management of multinational information systems. While certainly not comprehensive, some of the major issues include the emergence of integrated economies in Europe, the accelerating development of technology worldwide, the proliferation of electronic databases, and corporate concerns over intellectual property rights.

THE EMERGENCE OF REGIONAL ECONOMIES

The economies of the world's nation-states are undergoing a transformation that is driven by the globalization of commodity, consumer, industrial, and financial markets. One of the many intermediate steps toward a truly global economy is the emergence of regional trading blocs. In this section we discuss the information technology issues that are emerging as a result of the economic integration of Europe and the rapid shift of Eastern European countries to market-based economies.

The Economic Integration of Europe—EC 1992

In 1992 the first stage of economic integration for twelve European nations known as the European Community (EC) is expected to be completed. By 1993 more than 325 million European consumers will make up the largest single trading bloc in the world. The combined GNP of approximately $4.1 trillion is equivalent to that of the United States and is one and one-half times the size of Japan's economy. The major goal of Europe's economic integration is to eliminate internal trade barriers that now exist among neighboring countries so that goods, services, capital, labor, and information can freely cross national borders. The end result of the thousands of legal and regulatory changes that each country must adopt should be a business environment in which a product that is marketed and sold in one member country in accordance with the laws and regulation of that nation can be freely marketed, transported, and distributed in any other member country market.

There are several emerging issues in the economic integration of Europe that will have an impact on the management of information systems in multinational corporations doing business in Europe. The basic challenge for firms developing a strategic thrust into the EC is the problem of exploiting a larger market that will need comprehensive, timely, and accurate information. Figure 8–1 presents the key questions and tasks that must be addressed by the senior information systems managers of firms doing business in the European marketplace after 1992. Figure 8–2 presents a number of technical and managerial factors

---

What new needs will you have in the wider market for gathering, processing, and communicating information?

- Assess the information requirements of key aspects of your business such as marketing, sales, and distribution.
- Identify any business opportunities that need support.

Will you need new communication systems to support these requirements?

- Evaluate the telecommunications environment in each country you are considering.
- Evaluate public and private telecommunications services and tariffs.
- Investigate the benefit of using commercially available information services such as electronic data interchange, electronic mail, and access to databases.
- Consider what kinds of systems and applications your network will need to support.
- Investigate third-party networks and facilities management organizations.

How will you establish an information management function, keeping the following points in mind?

- Methods commonly used in the United States for data processing management do not apply.
- Skilled professionals are difficult to find.
- Telecommunications service can be unreliable.
- Managers utilize information differently than in the United States.

FIGURE 8–1   The Impact of EC 1992—Key Questions and Tasks

Source: Europe in the 1990s (New Jersey: KPMG Peat Marwick and the State of New Jersey, 1990), 29.

that need to be considered in developing strategies and plans that address the key questions and tasks.

Many U.S. companies are actively engaged doing business in Europe. Still others are preparing to enter the European market before 1992, anticipating that companies without a manufacturing presence in the EC will be at a competitive disadvantage. However, none of these firms, including large multinational corporations, anticipated the rapid changes now sweeping Eastern Europe. What are the information systems implications of an emerging market-based economy in Eastern Europe?

- Basic telecommunication service in Europe remains dominated by monopolized postal and telecommunications authorities.
- Generally, competition between value added service providers is allowed in Western Europe.
- By funding the RACE program for collaborative research in advanced communications technologies, initially the European Commission has concentrated its efforts on:
  — the development of common equipment standards in order to create a single European market for telecommunications terminal equipment
  — the need for Europe-wide services
  — the adoption of digital broadband technology
  — the creation of a common testing and certification center.
- Europe is five to nine hours ahead of the United States. This makes voice communication inconvenient.
- Mail costs between the U.S. and Europe can be surprisingly expensive and service slow.
- There is limited application software that functions on a Pan-European basis (e.g., meets accounting standards in all countries).
- A series of legislative initiatives has been launched with the aim of completely opening up the markets in telecommunications terminal equipment and in value added services. Other initiatives seek to lay down the conditions under which private operators and suppliers can have access to public contracts and public networks.

FIGURE 8-2   The Impact of EC 1992—Factors to Consider
Source: Europe in the 1990s (New Jersey: KPMG Peat Marwick and the State of New Jersey, 1990), 29.

The Emergence of Free Markets in Eastern Europe

Almost no one could have predicted the sudden and rapid changes that swept Eastern Europe in 1990. The failure of the central economies in Czechoslovakia, East Germany, Hungary, Poland, Yugoslavia, and the Soviet Union has pushed most of these countries to seek market-based restructuring solutions. Except for reunified East Germany and West Germany, each country is still trying to decide the correct approach to a market-based economy. Until these decisions are made and implemented, it is nearly impossible to speculate with any degree of certainty about the international technology issues that will emerge as a result. However, it is clear that two factors will influence Western firms doing business in Eastern Europe: a closer relationship with the EC countries and the lack of an information system infrastructure.

The economic integration of Western Europe will have a profound impact on Eastern Europe. Trade among Eastern European countries had taken place through an association of ten member nations called the Council for Mutual Economic Assistance (COMECON). COMECON used a five-year plan that enabled member countries to specialize in various export commodities, thus achieving low-cost production through specialization. Trade agreements through COMECON provided each country with needed imports. With the collapse of COMECON, there is no longer a large single market for Eastern European products. These countries must now actively look to Western markets for their exports and badly needed imports.

Over time, these countries will seek to join the EC or an equivalent trading association. The imperative for firms doing business in Eastern Europe is to view these operations over the long term as an extension of the EC. Many of the same information technology issues are beginning to surface in Eastern Europe. For example, data privacy protection is already an issue in Czechoslovakia and Hungary, with legislation pending before the government. Freedom of information is also a major issue in Eastern European nations because of the communist system's control over the rights of individual citizens.

A major shortcoming for Western firms doing business in Eastern Europe is the almost nonexistent telecommunications and data processing infrastructure. Establishing an infrastructure in Eastern Europe can be likened to establishing an information systems function in Third-World nations. It will take some time before the hardware, software, and human resources are comparable to the rest of Europe. Any information systems plan that includes Eastern Europe must allow for the integration of manual record-keeping systems and a realistic migration plan to advanced technologies that is appropriate to the skill level of the work force.

THE ACCELERATING DEVELOPMENT OF TECHNOLOGY

International information systems become viable through the development and integration of data processing technology and telecommunications technology. For decades, advancements in data processing technology have surpassed those in telecommunications. Today, this is no longer the case. A major obstacle to the development of global information systems is the cost of creating the telecommunications network. Capital requirements prohibit single organizations or countries from undertaking such efforts alone. The next generation of telecommunications infrastructures is being implemented through strategic alliances involving private corporations, government agencies, and quasi-government agencies. For example, INTELSAT was founded twenty-five years ago by a thirteen-country consortium. Its mission was to provide international public telecommunications services of high quality and reliability on a nondiscriminatory basis to all areas of the world and to contribute to world peace and understanding. INTELSAT now has 117 members and serves 173 countries with thirteen satellites providing over 116,000 full-time channels. In November 1989, INTELSAT VI was deployed. This four-story-high satellite with an in-orbit weight of three tons was the first of a new series of satellites being deployed through the joint investment of INTELSAT's member organizations.[2]

The world's telecommunications infrastructure is also growing undersea. The world's first transoceanic, fiber-optic cable capable of carrying 400,000 simultaneous telephone conversations between North America and Europe is the work of a strategic alliance between AT&T, France Telecom, and British Telecom. This new system, TAT-8, doubles the available capacity of existing transatlantic cables.[3]

Telecommunications infrastructure growth is not restricted to Europe and the United States. In the Association of Southeast Asian Nations (ASEAN) countries, there are current negotiations to develop a grand strategy for the deployment of a major undersea network of fiber-optic intraregional linkages and a regional satellite network. Southeast Asia represents the fastest growing ISDN network in the world, growing at an annual rate of 10 percent. For example, Singapore has added 400,000 new ISDN lines, while Taiwan has increased its system by 900,000 lines. Hong Kong has announced that it will have an all-digital network of 3 million lines by 1993.[4]

The capacity and capability of the world's telecommunications infrastructure is growing at an enormous rate because of strategic alliances. New systems are being targeted for specific regions and user groups. For example, EUTELSAT, a twenty-six country group, recently approved a Pan-European, medium-band broadcast satellite to be deployed in the mid-1990s. The satellite is the next generation of domestic direct broadcast systems equipped with seven overlapping beams to simultaneously cater to regional and linguistic markets.[5]

Some systems are industry-specific. IMMARSAT's Aeronautical Services Division plans to offer the international airline industry a low- and high-band data and voice telecommunications system for pilots and passengers. The system would enable passengers to carry personal telephones on board their flights and to connect their laptop computers to any computer system in the world for in-flight electronic mail transmission and data processing.[6]

The world's telecommunications infrastructure allows a corporation to link together every member of its organization anywhere in the world. The implications for the structure and organization of the firm are enormous. For example, the world's first network for interbank transfers was the Society for Worldwide Interbank Financial Telecommunications (SWIFT). For many years the system has provided simple message transmission for money transfers among its 2,900 members in sixty countries. Through the latest advancements in telecommunications technology, plans have been approved to develop SWIFT II. When it is on-line in the mid-1990s, this financial information system, based on the X.25 standard, will greatly expand the capabilities and services of member banks, enabling them to make file transfers in bulk and use interactive modes with store and forward functions.[7] The global telecommunications infrastructure not only has supported the operations of international banking but has changed the very nature of the banking business. The former Chairman of Citicorp, Walter Wriston, said in the early 1980s that money is information. In a global environment, the banks that handle information (money) most efficiently will make the most money (information).

The accelerating development of technology can be attributed to the economic development of many nations. Twenty years ago, the United States was almost the sole source of new technology. Today, many nations including Japan, Germany, France, and many others are making contributions that are expanding technology's frontiers and application around the world. Accompanying the growing ability to process and transmit information is the proliferation of data in the form of on-line databases.

GROWTH OF GLOBAL ON-LINE DATABASES

On-line databases containing in-depth and timely information are both a cause of and solution to the growing complexity of conducting business around the world. The international business environment is a twenty-four-hour-a-day arena in which access to the latest information can shift the competitive balance in the marketplace within minutes. Three emerging trends significantly affect the nature of international business and the manner in which firms manage their activities: (1) the proliferation of on-line databases, (2) the transborder accessibility to on-line data, and (3) the structure of on-line databases and related services.

Proliferation of On-line Databases

According to the Information Market Observatory (IMO) of the Commission of European Communities, the United States continues to lead the world in the production of on-line databases.[8] Database production is a major business opportunity for firms in service industries such as publishing and financial services. According to the IMO study, 56 percent of the databases produced and commercially available in 1987 were created in the United States. The EC accounted for just over one-fourth (27 percent) of the database production, with the remaining 17 percent produced in other developed countries such as Japan, South Korea, Canada, and Australia.

In Europe, Great Britain produces 32 percent of the commercially available on-line databases followed by Germany (18 percent), France (14 percent), Italy (11 percent), and Spain (10 percent). Interestingly, the growth in database production in Europe is 3 percent stronger than it is in the United States (16 percent versus 13 percent annual growth).

A major trend in the production of on-line databases is the dominance of for-profit versus nonprofit production. The U.S. market leads the world in for-profit database production, with almost 90 percent of the databases available for an access fee. In Europe the percentage is not as high, though there is a significant variation from country to country. For example, in Great Britain 68 percent of new on-line databases are produced by the private sector; in Germany the figure is 53 percent.

However, in contrast to Great Britain and Germany, more than 75 percent of the databases created in Spain, Italy, and Belgium come from public sectors. While database production in Asia is small in comparison to the United States and Europe, it is growing rapidly and is expected to account for a significant share of the data available through on-line services by the twenty-first century. Most likely, Japan will become the major producer of these databases.

Transborder Accessibility to On-line Data

In 1989 a West German researcher became the first user in a Western country to be granted a license by the Soviet Union to access the Soviet domestic data communication network. This East-West information link is one example of the trend to expand information accessibility. Today, many efforts are underway to create massive databases of scientific and technological information through the cooperation of governmental and quasi-governmental agencies and authorities. Information shared ranges from economic data to environmental and ecological data collected and stored within country borders. Many researchers believe that worldwide accessibility to these massive databases will enable researchers all over the world to work together in quasi-collaborative teams to solve many of the common problems facing all nations.

These benefits do not come without some major obstacles. For example, data definitions vary from country to country, cultural and sociological factors make data equivalence and comparability a problem, and a common interface to all the different systems does not yet exist.

The Changing Structure of On-line Databases and Services

An examination of the various types of on-line databases shows that these systems vary by country in terms of their purpose and structure. In the United States, most database production is geared to the end user. For example, databases provide users access to airline schedules, stock market quotations, and product catalogues. In Europe, most of the available databases are bibliographical in nature, providing title, abstract, and referral information only. The EC leads the world in the production of bibliographic databases while the United States is the dominant producer of factual, full-text databases. An emerging trend in commercial databases is the creation of a market for information. With accessibility to on-line databases in multiple countries, data have economic value like any other international commodity such as oil, wheat, or steel. The major impact of increased accessibility of data on multinational corporations is two fold. First, the increase in externally available data will require companies to make buy/build decisions regarding the firm's internal use of information. Second, greater access to information will increase the chances of conflicting, inaccurate, and irrelevant information being used by a firm's subsidiaries around the world. Increasingly, the global information resource management function will be to test for data accuracy, create methods of data comparability, and monitor the use of external databases.

Creators of databases for worldwide use will have to accommodate the needs of local users and, at the same time, standardize their database structures across cultures. For example, databases will become multilingual. Keywords and search criteria may be in English, but the user will typically require the text or body of data, as well as training and support services, to be in the native language.

INTELLECTUAL PROPERTY PROTECTION

As the flow of information around the world increases, the likelihood of misuse also grows. Multinational corporations seek to protect their intangible assets through patents, trademarks, and copyrights.[9] Various international conventions have attempted to standardize the process of international property protection and ensure that similar rights are enforced by host country governments in which the firm operates. For example, the Paris Union was established in 1883 to protect patents and trademarks in more than eighty countries, and the 1891 Madrid Agreement provided a central registration organization for patents and trademarks.

Computer software is protected by copyrights. Literary, musical, and artistic works are also covered by copyright protection. International copyright protection was established under two international conventions: the Berne Convention of 1886 and the Universal Copyright Convention of 1954. Unfortunately, even with the agreement of governments who were parties to the conventions, companies operating in the international environment suffer substantial copyright losses. Figure 8–3 presents a list of countries in which U.S.-based companies experienced most copyright infringement. In 1989 U.S. firms reported losses of approximately $1.5 billion in copyright infringements. Of the most-often cited sources of copyright infringement, Pacific Rim nations account for 76 percent of the total losses, or are eight of the top twelve transgressors.

Rank	*Country*	*Amount $ Million*
1	China	418
2	Saudi Arabia	189
3	South Korea	165
4	India	153
5	Phillipines	117
6	Taiwan	90
7	Indonesia	80
8	Brazil	68
9	Egypt	65
10	Thailand	61
11	Nigeria	39
12	Malaysia	32

FIGURE 8-3 U.S. Companies Copyright Losses in 1989 on Films, Music, Books, and Computer Software

Source: The International Intellectual Property Alliance, *Transnational Data and Communications Report* (Washington, DC: Transnational Data Reporting Service, December 1989), 20.

Intellectual property protection continues to be a major concern not only to software companies but also to any multinational company using its information systems applications portfolio to gain a competitive advantage in overseas countries.

SUMMARY

In this book we have discussed two important trends that are transforming the environment of business and the practice of management: the globalization of markets and the impact of information technology on the firm. The important link between these trends is information. Information is power to the government, corporation, or manager that is able to harness it to achieve its goals. For privacy and economic reasons, governments are increasingly concerned about the flow of information and the implications of technology advancement for their society. Host country governments want to develop their own information infrastructure without dependence on foreign companies and governments. Many governments see data as a resource like any natural resource such as oil, coal, or timber. Without an advanced information technology infrastructure, they fear becoming Third-World exporters of raw data and importers of value added information products and services. Multinational corporations continue to seek ways to leverage their significant investments in information technology to gain competitive advantage in the world market, while managers seek access to real-time information in order to manage and coordinate organizations that span the globe.

In this chapter we highlighted the growing interaction of markets around the world and the trend toward economic regionalization in Europe and Asia. An important characteristic of this economic integration is the need for businesses to coordinate the flow of goods and services across national borders. In response to society's needs, governments and corporations are rapidly expanding the capabilities of their information technology infrastructure. This requires a high level of coordination and communication between the entities. However, because of differing goals, governments and corporations often conflict with each other over the pace and direction of information technology deployment. It is not hard to understand why these issues are growing in importance; after all, information is the lifeblood of international business and information technologies are the organs that drive it through the world marketplace.

As you complete this text, we hope that you will reflect on the major issues presented. The international dimensions of information systems and technology will be increasingly important to businesses and managers if they want continued success in the twenty-first century.

NOTES

1. Arno Penzias, *Ideas and Information* (New York: W. W. Norton & Company, 1989), 206.

2. *Transnational Data and Communications Report* (Washington, DC: Transnational Data Reporting Service, Inc., October 1989), 5.

3. *Transnational Data and Communications Report* (Washington, DC: Transnational Data Reporting Service, Inc., January 1989), 3.

4. *Transnational Data and Communications Report* (Washington, DC: Transnational Data Reporting Service. Inc., February 1989) 3.

5. *Transnational Data and Communications Report* (Washington, DC: Transnational Data Reporting Service, Inc., January 1989), 4.

6. *Transnational Data and Communications Report* (Washington, DC: Transnational Data Reporting Service, Inc., March 1989). 4.

7. *Transnational Data and Communications Report* (Washington, DC: Transnational Data Reporting Service, Inc., April 1989), 8.

8. Transnational Data and Communications Report (Washington, DC: Transnational Data Reporting Service, Inc., December 1989), 9.

9. Michael Litka, *International Dimensions of the Legal Environment of Business* (Boston: PWS-Kent Publishing Co., 1988).

STUDY QUESTIONS

1. What key issues and tasks should senior information systems executives consider regarding the impact of the EC 1992 plan?

2. What are the forces driving the accelerated pace of technology development?

3. If you were the senior IS executive of a company and the president of that firm asked you to speculate on the emerging IS issues in Eastern Europe, what would you say?

4. Given the accelerating pace of technology, will it be possible for Eastern European countries to develop an information systems infrastructure that is competitive with the EC? Discuss your point of view.

5. What additional issues do you think will influence the direction that information systems and technology will follow as we enter the twenty-first century?

SUGGESTED READINGS

Dennis, Alan R., et al. "A New Role for Computers in Strategic Management," *Journal of Business Strategy* (September–October 1990): 38–43.

Donaldson, Thomas. *The Ethics of International Business.* New York: Oxford University Press, 1989.

Dudley, James W. *1992: Strategies for the Single Market.* Massachusetts: Productivity Press, 1989.

"The Incredible Shrinking Company," *The Economist* (December 15, 1990): 65–66.

Nasbitt, John and Patricia Aburdene. *Ten New Directions for the 1990s: Megatrends 2000.* New York: William Morrow & Co., 1990.

Ohmae, Kenichi. *The Borderless World: Power and Strategy in the Interlinked Economy.* New York: Harper Business, 1990.

———. *Beyond National Borders: Reflections on Japan and the World.* Homewood, IL: Dow Jones-Irwin, 1987.

Penzias, Arno. *Ideas and Information: Managing in a High-Tech World.* New York: W. W. Norton & Co., 1989.

Index